IN THIS CITY,
WE DANCE

DONALD E.
DUKES

IN THIS CITY, WE DANCE

A Nexphrase Book / published by arrangement
with the author

For information, address: Nexphrase Publishing
9337 Salina Way, Sacramento, CA 95827

ISBN: 0-9653638-0-5

Library of Congress Catalog Card Number:
96-97032

PRINTED IN THE UNITED STATES OF AMERICA

6-9-9?

Dedicated to my mother,
Dorothy Finis Dukes

To Marie: This
book is to a person
whom I've just met
but feel like I've
known for ages

Acknowledgments.

The success of this book is a testament of the love and faith of my mother, Dorothy Finis Dukes who died February 10, 1996. She left a legacy of love and caring the world will sorely miss. And I miss her most of all.

The purpose of this book is to give tribute to the men and women who have gone unsung but have maintained their loyalty and faith in their people.

I want to thank and acknowledge that, without the help and encouragement of Brenda Usher, this work might still be sitting on the shelf. Her family and their love have given me new strength and insight of the needs and particularities in the African Personality.

Thank luck or faith that I was introduced to Bill Jones, the photographer whose expertise and patience allowed me to develop the appropriate cover. Also thank luck or faith that allowed me to meet and work with Jim Reid who set up the design and was the finish editor of this work. I would like to thank Ruth Ellison for reading the manuscript and making many helpful suggestions. Thank my father, who not only supported me for a limited time while my finances went into the book, but also contributed financially.

Thank my nephew, Stephan Saunders whose business sense allowed me to make correct decisions and encouraged me with the publishing of the book.

For all those subversive forces, thank you for establishing the dialectical need for protracted struggle in all phases of human development.

I acknowledge the spiritual forces that are always at work, strongly, under the surface of all motion and matter — it has chosen that I be successful in this venture, and I'm grateful.

IN THIS CITY, WE DANCE

Arms outstretched, bathed in purple stage lights, Thelma looked out into the audience. A sizzling tune by Chaka Khan eased her body into the throbbing tempo. Thelma felt the stage lights cascading off of her legs and arms. The pulsating bass drum beat its way from the pit of her stomach into her shoulders and hips. She strutted center stage, catching the top of the funky bass with her hips and brought it crashing down upon the audience. Her cat eyes glittered, beads of sweat flowed down her brown thighs onto the floor. She began her strip — tedious, and intoxicating. She arched her back and swiveled on the toes of her high heels. The routine became an art form. The audience was dazed — transfixed into a pungent web of sexual energy.

Tossing her head, she became raunchy. Thelma bent down, swinging and contorting her buttocks. The crowd swayed with her. At the end of her routine, Thelma spun and gracefully left the stage.

Thelma's expression, in the murky light off stage, showed a sense of satisfaction. She wallowed in it, enjoying the feel of control. The applause rebounded and resounded off the dingy walls. Catcalls and pleas for her returned performance followed her off stage. She could still hear them shouting her name while she sat spent in her dressing room.

"That was *real* girl. You knocked 'em dead!" Jackie exclaimed.

Thelma was looking in her makeup mirror trying to spot any grey hairs. There were none. She absentmindedly nodded her head.

Jackie, another stripper was a six foot two amazon. Her smooth yellow complexion and high cheeks gave her an African-Oriental look.

"Well, I'm up next," she said, standing and looking into Thelma's mirror to touch up her hair.

"What do you have planned for tonight?" she asked.

"I plan to go home and curl up with a good book," Thelma replied.

"You should get out more. This ain't all life got to offer you know," Jackie said.

"Well, what are you going to do tonight, Jackie?"

"There's a party over at Pinballs and you know it will be live and goin' on," she replied.

"I'll pass for tonight. Plus, dope boys just don't suit my cup of tea," Thelma responded.

"You ain't got to be bothered with him or his crew. You might even meet somebody nice," Jackie said.

There was a soft knock on the door.

"Everybody decent?" a man's voice asked.

"Yeah, come on in," Jackie answered.

A short brown skinned man with a close clipped afro stepped into the dressing room. It was Phats, the stage manager.

"Baby, you trying to hurt someone?" he asked Jackie, taking a step back. "You could cause severe accidents on deserted streets in that outfit."

Both woman broke into laughter. Jackie was dressed in her Daisy Dukes shorts, halter, and spiked heels.

He said, "Jackie you're up. You got thirty seconds."

"I'm gone, if you change your mind Thelma, beep me." She turned and disappeared into the hall.

Phats turned out to be a friend to the girls that danced at the hall. He was married and treated all the girls with the utmost of respect. Thelma had even begun to like Phats. He minded his business and didn't take no stuff even off Mr. Newvel, the owner of the club.

Phats lingered around the dressing room. "What's on your mind, Phats?" Thelma asked.

"I've been in this business for over forty-years. In fact, I met my wife here. There have been a lot of girls come and go, some with talent some with not so much talent. But you Thelma, you're special. You are an artist. You capture something that has been in our societies since antiquity. Not since Madam Z have I seen anyone capture the audience the way you do. *Women* have started to come see you!" he said.

"The only advice I can offer you is to pay off your debts, then just disappear. Leave this business and don't even look back."

He patted her on the shoulder and walked out of the dressing without a backward glance.

Later, while on the subway, Thelma watched the lights of the city whiz past her from the darkness. Lately, she had felt a heaviness around her. Cautious by nature, Thelma had become almost paranoid this last week. Phats would not have told her that unless he knew something concrete.

The glittering lights of the city began to fade with the rays of the sun bouncing off the concrete and steel buildings. When she got off at her stop, working people carrying lunch pails and shopping bags were scurrying toward the subway. Everyone seemed serious this time of the morning, she thought, unlike the afternoon crowd where there was laughter and loud brazen greetings.

Everybody trying to get money. However you got it, you had to have it. Nobody asked where it came from. It was something that you had to have. It seemed that this society turned everyone into some type of thief. Just, some types of thieving were more acceptable then others. Crabs in a barrel, she thought.

Thelma shook herself. "I can't save the world. I can't even save myself," her mind whirled.

I'll call my homey, Tiffenie. She hurried into her apartment, throwing her duffel bag and purse on the couch. She dialed Tiffenie's number.

Tiffenie stood on her 'early morning furry rug'. She curled her toes into its softness. She loved luxury no matter how inconvenient. It was what life was all about. Tiffenie was just finishing up the last layer of makeup when she heard her phone ring. Tipping into her living room, she said aloud, "This can't be nobody but Thelma." "What did you do this time, you little hussy," she answered, before allowing for a greeting.

"Girl, one of these times you goin' to answer the phone and it ain't goin' to be me." Thelma paused, then said, "Then even I won't be able to save you."

Both women giggled. "Tiff, I knew that you would cheer me up," Thelma's voice becoming serious.

"You sound a little down. What's up, seriously," Tiffenie asked, concern in her voice.

"I was just feeling real frustrated and down. I knew your crazy self would cheer me up," Thelma answered.

Tiffenie glanced at her wall clock with the portrait of Malcolm X embedded on the face.

"I got a few minutes, Thelma." Tiffenie changed her voice to Ms. Gangster. "You know," she began, mocking seriousness. "If somebody messing with my girl, you know that I got to do 'im. What he look like? You know I like 'em bowlegged with a attitude."

Thelma had to snatch the phone from her ear or be deafened by the peals of laughter coming from Tiffenie. "Girl, I be playin' sometime, but at this juncture, I really do believe you is crazy," Thelma began laughing despite herself. "Go to work nut, and call me when you get off," Thelma shouted through the laughter.

"I got to go, but let's do lunch this coming Friday. You saved me, Thelma. I'll go all the way for you," Tiffenie stated, her voice again serious.

"It ain't all that — I just needed to hear a friend's voice," said Thelma.

Tiffenie hung up the phone. It was a promise that she and Thelma had made to each other. Be real. Be a friend. And never would they make excuses to each other for being themselves.

Tiffenie tipped into her bathroom, her flesh jiggling. Her blue black complexion shone. I'm going to have to loose some of this weight, she thought. Michael, her high school sweetheart, had loved her ample hips, thighs, and breasts. Tiffenie surveyed her figure in the full length mirror. Men of all nationalities simply went mad over her full figure. Yeah, she thought, I haven't had a man of any kind in over a year and a half.

On the subway she began her transformation. Her almond shaped eyes narrowed into unfeeling slits. Her usual radiant smile would now become 'corporate plastic.'

Tiffenie got off at the Branet Wind Way stop. She had to walk two blocks to get to her office building. The city's largest bus station was located in the last block. It was here that a lot of men lounged around. Most of them were Black.

Some of them were dressed casually — well groomed with freshly cut hair and trimmed beards. Others were, or looked like bums, unshaven, and dirty. But all of them had that gleam in their eyes.

Today, she sensed someone watching her intently. Tiffenie walked faster, her heart pounding, her gait strong and purposeful.

"Hey, psst..." A man approached her.

She almost tripped over her own feet. He looked so much like her brother. Stan was somewhere in Philly still strung out on drugs.

"Hey fine woman, I just wanted to say hi."

Tiffenie whirled around to face him. "What do you want?" she asked sharply.

He laughed almost like her brother. "Just wanted to greet the finest Black woman I've seen since puberty," he stated, his eyes laughing.

"Well hello," she replied. Tiffenie turned and walked briskly to her office building.

Another world awaited her as she entered the smoked glass revolving doors. She left the elevator that took her to the modern office complex where she put in her daily eight. "Good morning, Mrs. Pitney." Tiffenie greeted the aging secretary.

"Oh, hello, Mrs. Watkins, and how was your weekend?" she asked without looking away from her computer.

Before Tiffenie could find a suitable answer, Mrs. Pitney added, "You have four messages which are on your desk and Mr. Rosenthal would like to see you."

Tiffenie, with a nod of her head, briskly entered her office which had a view that overlooked the east side of the city. The sunlight that was beginning to flood her office did little to warm her.

She flicked on her computer while going through her office mail. As the main instrument of her work began warming up for its endless rows of names and account numbers, Tiffenie pressed a red button at the lower left side of her desk.

Lowering her lips to the intercom, she stated in a clipped voice, "Oh Mrs. Pitney, tell Mr. Rosenthal that I'm ready to see him if he's not too busy."

"He just got in, Ms. Watkins. He'll see you in about ten minutes," Mrs. Pitney answered.

Tiffenie swiveled her chair around to face the window. She rose and opened the venetian blinds to watch the scene below.

From her eleventh floor window she could see the entire parking lot begin to fill with those nine to five rush hour folks. As the sun rose, its rays began to burn through the morning mist from the city. Two sparrows in the shade of a red BMW caught her wandering gaze. Positioned like book ends, one would hop sideways three jerky hops, the other bird would mimic the first. This went on in a delicate pattern until the birds simultaneously flew away in a burst of brown and white feathers.

Wistfully, Tiffenie thought of Michael, her sweetheart from high school. They had also attended the same college. Michael had only lasted one quarter. Pressure from her peers and parents had forced Tiffenie to drop Michael for something better. Tiffenie wondered if the dull ache that gripped her when she thought of him was something better.

Tiffenie snapped out of her daydreaming. Mr. Rosenthal didn't like to be kept waiting. Walking the length of the plush carpeted floor toward Mr. Rosenthal's office, a slight tug of uncertainty could be detected through her professional exterior.

Mr. Rosenthal, seated at a ponderous oak desk, answered the quiet knock with a gruff, "Come on in, will ya?"

Tiffenie strode into the office, then hesitated,

"Sit down. Rest yourself," Rosenthal stated.

He positioned his eyes on her midriff and watched her form slide into full view as she seated herself in the chair facing his desk.

"You wanted to see me?" Tiffenie asked, sitting, her back stiff as a board.

"Well, Ms. Watkins, I'm more then pleased with your performance with our company. But as you know, sales personnel have to make a point of getting to know their fellow employees a little bit better." He bit the word better between his lip and tongue.

Tiffenie's eyes shone brightly. She relaxed and allowed herself to get a good look at this Mr. Rosenthal.

His hands were laced over a middle-aged punch which seldom saw the need for exercise; his shirt was rolled up to reveal thick hairy forearms.

She replied, "If you mean getting to know some of the staff a little bit better, I will make a point of it." She bit the word better between her lip and tongue and continued. "I'm really sorry that I could not make the big sales party last month, but I had relatives visiting."

Rosenthal, not lost on the hint of sarcasm, arched his eyebrows. He laughed a short bullish sound, that was to Tiffenie, a poor substitute for any display of humor.

"Well, Ms. Watkins, as long as we have some type of understanding..." he paused.

"If that is all, Mr. Rosenthal, I have a ton of work to get out," Tiffenie interjected and began to rise.

"Let's make a deal." His voice had taken on a more soothing tone.

"Yes, what's that," Tiffenie said cautiously.

"You call me Jim and I'll call you Tiffenie. Is that a deal?" he asked, amused at her discomfort.

"That's fine, Mr...", Tiffenie caught herself, "Jim."

He fabricated a grin and said, "That will be all ,Tiffenie."

She rose and walked to the door. That day she had worn her off-white knit business suit — it melted to every curve of her body. She felt his gaze on her hips as she exited his office.

While back in her office, Tiffenie thought of the birds courting in the shade of the parking lot. For the life of her she could not understand why those birds reminded her of her relationship with Michael. She could not go on with this isolation. Thelma had helped, but she still needed more. Tiffenie wondered what her mother was doing. Probably working on her garden. Her parents were very proud of her — she had worked very hard in college.

"Wonder what Judy is doing?" she asked herself aloud. The last time she had talked to her best friend from college, she was so excited about the new furniture that she and her husband were purchasing. Her husband had also secured a new coaching position. Tiffenie did not have the nerve to tell Judy that her husband had propositioned her on their wedding day. He had even made a passes at her whenever he answered the phone when she called. It all seemed so meaningless.

She toyed with the idea of calling Judy, but that was not exactly what she wanted to do. "Hmmm, I wonder if Thelma's awake," she asked aloud.

he rays of the mid-afternoon sun caught Thelma's honey toned complexion snuggled against plaid designed gray and black pillow cases. Her tranquil form was languished across her rolled out sleeper. Suddenly, her form tensed and a muffled cry escaped from her lips. This is how she woke to the afternoon sun.

The stinging pellets of hot water helped to return her to the waking world. She began singing a tune by Toni Braxton, 'Seven Whole Days'. Thelma became so engrossed in the revitalizing shower and song that she almost missed the shrill ringing of the phone.

Wet and dripping, clutching a terry cloth robe around her, "Hello. Good afternoon," she answered.

"Hey sleepy head, this is Tiffenie. Did I wake you?"

"Naw. I was taking a shower. This is a surprise — nobody calls me this time of the day except my manager. And if you knew him he ain't never got to call," she answered.

There was a long pause, Thelma sensed something was wrong. "What's up, Tiff?" Another pause.

"I had to call somebody, Thelma. Somebody who I knows cares. I just needed somebody to say hi to. You know?"

"I'm glad you called ,girlfriend. It's nice to be needed and thought of," Thelma replied.

"This isolation is really getting to me," Tiffenie said.

"You know what?" Thelma asked.

"What," Tiffenie answered.

"We need to go out and party. I haven't been out in ages," Thelma said.

"That sounds like the best thing I've heard in a while," Tiffenie stated.

"Let's see, the weekends are my money nights so let's go out this coming Thursday. How is that for your schedule?" Thelma asked.

"That's a bet, Thelma, but what are you doing tonight before you go into work," Tiffenie asked.

"Stop through when you get off from work," Thelma replied.

"OK. See you about six," Tiffenie replied.

Thelma stood for a moment holding the phone in her hand listening to the dial tone. Then she completed her shower.

BROTHERHOOD

 4

T he old Camero stood askew, one side lifted up off the ground by building blocks. A man's head was submerged in the gaping mouth of the lifted hood. He shouted to another man whose feet were sticking out from under the car, "You ready? This pipe is getting heavy."

"Come on with it," the man under the car answered.

With a unified push and tug the tubing connecting the muffler to the automobile was joined and secured into place by a metal clamp.

Raising his head from the depths of the hood while wiping his hands with a rag, the man standing said, "That should hold you ,Jason."

Jason, a slimmer man by comparison, wiggled from under the narrow confines and stood by the heavier man to appraise the work.

"Yeah. How much do I owe you, man?" Jason asked, while digging into the tattered pockets of his jeans.

Jomo was sweating from the labor and the bright spring sun. He shrugged his muscular shoulders and answered, "You don't owe me nuthin'. Just when I need a favor, I know that you'll come through."

Jason slapped his friend on the shoulder. Eyeing him intently from the corner of his eye, he replied, "Yeah, we partners ,Jomo, and you know that I will help you if I can. But dig this, I ain't no fan."

Jomo threw his head to one side letting his heavy knit dredlocks spring back and forth. This was his silent version of laughter.

"Look at my old homeboy getting a little nervous at the
company he's keeping," he said.

Jason and Jomo had known each other since the first
grade. It was not what you said to make Jason angry, it
was the tone of voice that was used. He mimicked Jason's
father when he was scolding him. That made Jason wince.
He and Jomo looked at each other and broke out in gales
of laughter.

"There is nothing that can replace an old friend, Jomo,"
he said.

"We buddies from way back — nothing can harm that,
man. You stuck with me when my mom died. I'll always
remember that." Jomo replied.

Jason gave Jomo one of his rare smiles. "They still hir-
ing at Dinks Security. If you would give it a chance I,
could get them to hire you," Jason stated.

"Come on mon, if I want to work for charity, I'll go all
the way and work for the Salvation Army. Do you know
how much I make in a single drop?" He asked bitterly. He
paused, walked two steps away from Jason, and walked
back to his original position.

"Look mon, we been through this, Jason. I don't like
what I'm doing, but at least I don't have to kiss somebod-
ies ass for a check that does not allow me to live decently."

Jason surveyed his friend Jomo thoughtfully, he finally
said, "OK man, just trying to give you some other alternatives." Glancing at his watch he continued, "Meet you at
Dotty's tonight, and don't forget we going to that Rhasta
party Thursday."

Waving from his beat up Camero, Jason shouted, "See
you about nine."

Jason switched on his street blaster as he entered his
one room flat. In the shower, the stinging wet rays of

water glided him into a state of oblivion. He thought of Jomo. They had lived just a few blocks away as kids. They were teammates on the winning state football team. He remembered the block that Jomo had thrown that had allowed him to enter into the end zone with the winning touchdown. High school was another world from the one they were thrown into after graduation.

He had joined the Marine Corps and Jomo had joined the Scorpios, a reputed street gang. They both had killed people they had no business killing.

Desert Storm was the biggest joke. That so-called war would be characterized as the biggest waste in history. They transported so much equipment and supplies, that it was cheaper to leave millions of dollars worth of stuff there after the war rather then ship it back to the States. For the price of one of those tanks, he could have a decent paying job. The issue now was to find a "real job." This security shit was for the birds. He wasn't sure how long he would last. And to think of it — him telling Jomo to work with him at $6.75 per hour. He even laughed at his pay check when Friday rolled around. Well, at least he didn't have to always look over his shoulder. That was something that he had noticed that Jomo did nowadays.

He had also noticed that a large population of Arabs from Saudi Arabia resembled Brothers from L.A., Harlem, Toledo, and even those Brothers from Detroit.

The white G.I.'s always had jokes concerning the Arabs. Many of the jokes were simple, newer versions of old nigga jokes. He began to feel like he had wrongly invaded somebody's turf.

Jason began having the same dream over and over again once he got back to the states. While in Saudi Arabia, he was sent with fifty other men to lay down a line of fire from some bunkers in the front lines. It was pitch

black. Rocket, missile and artillery shells were going off
in every direction, giving him a bird's eye view of a spec-
tacular demonstration of man's destructive capabilities. It
was the mother of all Fourths of July. Somebody fucked
up. Either somebody gave the wrong coordinates or somebody at the other end misinterpreted. American artillery
dropped a barrage of shells into the bunker where he and
fifty men were stationed for night observation. The result
was thirty-five men killed and ten seriously injured.
Jason was unharmed, not even a scratch. The experience
tore Jason apart mentally and emotionally. The maimed
carcasses and the blood which drenched Jason caused him
to have nightmares even to this day.

Jason's commanding officer was a stone racist from
somewhere in the jungles of Boston. Brothers were always
the ones he made dig the latrines, and he was free with
his racial slurs. That bothered Jason. What really shocked
him was, while out on night patrol, he witnessed two
white G.I.'s rape and kill a young Arab girl.

After the soldier had coolly shot her in the head, he
slapped Jason on the shoulder and said, "Now ain't
nuthin' wrong with getting a little poontang. Is it?"

In a scant second, a young Arab boy appeared like a
shadow and cut both men down in mid-stride. His machine gun still smoldering, he looked at Jason with a
hypnotic stare and asked, "Why are you here in this land?
You should be fighting in your own land for your own
people."

He disappeared into the shadows from which he had
materialized. Jason made his way back to the main body
of troops. He was never asked about the two men, and the
bodies were never found.

Jason's remaining stint in Saudi Arabia was like a slow
nightmare. It seemed that endless desert, poor food, and

the brown and green colors of the uniforms were the beginning and end of the world.

After almost a year he returned to the states. His adjustment period, or at least that's what the shrinks in the military called it, was a nightmare of a different sort.

Jason had lived with his parents all of his life. Now they seemed alien. After greeting his parents at the airport with the customary hugs and kisses, he was unsure of what to say.

He and his father used to watch westerns together. Jason tried it one night just to spend some time with his father, but he could no longer digest the idea that the Indians were the bad guys and the settlers were the good guys.

"Them settlers was a muthafucka," he mumbled to himself one night, while watching westerns with his old man.

"What's that ,Jason?" his father had asked.

"For a long time ,Dad, I really thought that the Indians were the bad guys and the white guys were the good guys. Now that I know that Europeans murdered all the Indians in the Caribbean and they wiped out most of the Indians in the far eastern states of this country. Now they got the rest of them on plantations called reservations. I know better." He paused. Never had he talked to his father about politics. He continued, "It's an insult to my intelligence, and I'm ashamed that I had been tricked in to believing that these wars in other countries would preserve our freedom, Daddy." He had not called his father Daddy in years. He stood and faced his father who was sitting in his usual easy chair.

"I feel like a fool. Here I am, the big bad GI who came to get it together for the peoples of Saudi Arabia, and those people didn't even want us over there. The way the sol-

diers treated the Arabs, the way some of the Arabs
treated the Africans, is the way that we're treated here.

"I was tricked so good ,Daddy, that when I envisioned
America, I envisioned television world. Not this world, not
this neighborhood where we live." Jason's eyes were
shining, and a thin film of sweat had materialized on his
forehead.

"We're all Americans, son. You'd better let all that hate
and old slavery stuff go. Ain't nothing you can do about it
but just get along," his father said, standing and facing
him.

"If this is what America's got to offer, I got to find something better or make it better. I owe it to you, mother,
myself, and Black people in general!" Jason shouted. He
noticed that his hands were shaking.

"Son, you're excited and you're still recovering from your
tour in Saudi Arabia. Let's talk about this in the morning," his father had said, soothingly.

"Why didn't you tell me the truth, Daddy? Why did you
let me believe all of those lies?" Jason shouted.

"Look son, you're not going to call me a liar in my own
house. What you need to do is to quit reading all those
hate books and go get you a college education."

Jason abruptly left the house, slamming the door behind
him. That night, he dreamed of barrages of artillery
mangled corpses and being drenched in blood. At the end
of the dream, he was violently fighting camouflaged figures who were trying to bury him. His screech woke his
parents. Jason sat dumbfounded when his father told him
that he would have to leave the house. "Find somewhere
else to live," he had stated, matter-of-factly.

Jason was angry at his father. After a few days, he
began to feel a new type of freedom. No parents, no military, just him.

Across town, about the same time that Jason was on his way to work, Jomo dialed a memorized phone number from a pay phone. A man owning a swank bachelors apartment answered his expensive French phone saying, "Yeah, this is Walter. Yeah, Jomo, meet you here a seven sharp."

J ust before leaving her office, Tiffenie decided that the crowded subway would be a bit too much. Instead of rushing out of the building like she and fifteen hundred other employees usually did, she called a taxi, and made some new entries on her computerized Rollodex to kill some time. While standing in the lobby, just inside the smoky-grey revolving doors, Tiffenie noticed a new guard stationed at the front desk.

Their eyes met innocently enough. Jason was thumbing through an ancient Black World magazine. She smiled and caught him off guard. Tiffenie turned to see if her taxi had arrived. Jason's gaze fell on the havoc that her ample hips were making on that clinging knit suit.

She turned and said, "I haven't seen you before. Are you new?"

"No, I've been working at this post for almost six months. You probably haven't seen me because your shift leaves before I get here. Are you working overtime or something?" he asked.

She pursed her lips. "No, not really. I just didn't feel like riding the subway."

"If you called a cab, I believe your ride has arrived," he said.

Tiffenie turned to see a green and white cab nestled close to the curb. "Yes, I believe that's for me. Thanks, and it was nice meeting you," she added before leaving.

Jason was spellbound as he watched her until she disappeared into the taxi. I can barely take care of myself let alone a woman like her, he thought bitterly to himself.

Thelma answered the door dressed in a faded blue jogging suit. Before Tiffenie could open her mouth, Thelma said, "What they do, kick your ass for lunch? You look like you've had a heck of a day. Make yourself comfortable I want to hear all about it. Before you get started, let me get our drinks."

Tiffenie stretched herself out on the overstuffed easy chair while Thelma retrieved the icy red dacrya from the freezer.

"What's been goin' on with you, girlfriend?" Tiffenie asked.

"Same old stuff, girlfriend — dancing and sleeping," she answered, emerging from the kitchen. Thelma handed Tiffenie a large red goblet, then seated herself on a stool directly across from her.

The room settled on an uncomfortable silence. Tiffenie took a loud sip of her drink, "Mmmm, that's good. Just what I needed."

Tiffenie, toying with her straw said, "If I ask you a question, will you answer me as best you can?"

"Yeah, why not," Thelma replied.

"If you suddenly look around you and all the things that you thought meant something to you are no longer important or meaningful, what is the next step"?

"Girl, who is you asking?" Thelma replied. "Look, Tiffenie, I don't know what you're going though, but at least you got a job that can take you places. You got money, a nice place, and shoot, you might even meet a man."

"I've heard that shit so many times and it ain't shit to even think about," she replied angrily.

"Look Tiffenie," Thelma sat her glass down and stood. "Everybody goes through a point in their life when they question what's important or try to find out exactly what

they're supposed to be doing. That's natural. Now I hear
this growing agitation coming out of you. Yo baby, I'm
angry. I think that you got it made in the shade, and you
crying. At least you got a mamma and daddy. They even
think to call you. I ain't got nothing nor nobody. At least
you had a relationship with somebody. I'm not sure if I
know what a relationship is with a man. You know what?"
She paused, took a gulp from her drink and continued,
"I'm so fucked up, I'm scared to have somebody. Men tell
me I'm fine twenty times a day before I get to work. Girl
friend," she screamed. "I ain't had a man in almost a
year!"

Tiffenie stood. An uninformed spectator would have
thought that a fist fight was about to break out.

"I don't give a flying flip, Thelma, of what I got. Bottom
line is that I'm not happy. I'm alone and afraid. Living
like this cannot be all that life has to offer. And yeah,
Thelma, I'm mad as hell."

Thelma grasped her drink, spilling a bit on the hard
wood floor. "Hear, hear! A salute and toast to all the evil
Black bitches this side of the Mississippi."

"Salute!" Tiffenie shouted.

The two women, standing, looked each other in the eye,
clashed their glasses together and drank deeply. In the
background, the lyrics of Stevie Wonder's hit record,
'Living for the City', filled the apartment. After the record
ended, the spell lifted.

Tiffenie, a little tipsy, said, "Got to go. I have to get up
tomorrow."

"Remember, we goin' partying tomorrow night," Thelma
reminded, closing the door behind her retreating back.

The next day, Tiffenie stayed after work with the excuse
that she needed to catch up on some work. She waited a

half hour before taking the elevator down to the front lobby.

Jason was sitting at the desk that faced the door. He was reading.

The tapping of her heels on the floor brought his head from the depths of the book.

"Hello," he greeted.

"Well, hello to you," Tiffenie replied. "I didn't introduce myself yesterday, I'm Tiffenie."

Jason tried to stand but bumped his knees on the desk. "My name is Jason," he replied, extending his hand, remaining seated. Her hand felt warm and alive in his grasp.

He was at a loss for what to say. She removed her hand from his after she realized that they had been holding hands and staring.

"Looks like you're trying to make all the money staying overtime again," he stated.

Tiffenie thought it would not be in good taste to explain to him that she was a salaried employee.

"No, just trying to stay ahead. I have a lot of work," she replied.

"Are you waiting on your cab?" he asked, looking past her into the street.

Tiffenie realized that she hadn't called a taxi. She had forgotten.

"You know I forgot to call one. May I use your phone?"

"Certainly. I'll dial the number for you."

After she talked to the dispatcher, she handed the phone back to Jason. Their hands brushed in the exchange.

"I noticed that you're always reading. Are you in school or something."

"No, I'm not in school. I just read a lot. I don't enjoy watching TV, and I don't go out much. How about you?

What do you do in your spare time?" he asked, managing to stand without his knees getting in the way.

"I just work... and go home and work," she answered thoughtfully.

"Maybe we can do a movie sometime," he stated, surprised at the ease in which he had asked her.

"That would be nice, Jason," she answered.

At that time the taxi rolled up to the curb. "That's my cab, Jason. Here is my home number. Don't lose it," she added, before pushing her way through the revolving grey doors.

The humidity with the heat of the day settled over the city. The exhaust fumes from the stream of traffic made breathing a chore.

Once in her apartment, Tiffenie remembered that she and Thelma had a date. She couldn't remember the last time that she had gone out. "Hmmm... What can I wear for tonight?" She was becoming excited. At length, she choose a black silk dress that accented her full breasts. The cleavage ran almost to her navel. Its length stopped an inch above her knees. Black stockings and heels. She twirled around in front of her floor length mirror. Tiffenie thought she looked enticing.

It was a Thursday night and the city had begun to hum with the thought of the approaching weekend. Any night that was party night for working folks, was a night to forget unpaid bills, degrading working environments, or anything that could be considered a problem. Tonight was a night to forget one's troubles and lose oneself in the rhythm of life.

Thelma answered Tiffenie's knock wearing a blue terrycloth robe. In her left hand, was a lip stick tube.

"Whew girl, you out to seriously attract some attention ain't you!" Thelma exclaimed, grinning.

Tiffenie spun gracefully on her tiptoes. "How come you're not ready, I haven't been out in a decade and, as you can see, I'm hot to trot."

"Calm down ,girl, the party won't be swinging until eleven. We're going to happy hour first. So just sit your country self down." Reaching into a tray under her coffee table, she withdrew an unevenly rolled cigarette. "Here, smoke a little of this until I'm finished with my shower."

Thelma emerged from the bathroom smelling of something rich and sassy. Her cornrows were lavishly rolled to one side of her head giving her a regal appearance. Her silk dress was adorned with a large, white flower on the front. Unlike Tiffenie's, her dress covered her neck in a chic tight collar. The curve of her perfectly proportioned hips and melon shaped breasts were accented. The dress fit like a second skin.

Spinning on her toes for Tiffenie's benefit, she asked, "Am I ready ,girlfriend?"

"Yeah, let's knock 'em dead," Tiffenie responded.

The club that Thelma had in mind was located in the business district of downtown. The bar ran in a semicircle in the center of the club. It was the hangout of the well-to-do and up-and-coming executive set. This was the first time that either women had been there.

Standing at the entrance, Tiffenie felt quite bold and excited. The few puffs of reefer that Thelma had taken had given her a sense of confidence she usually did not feel in a unfamiliar environment. While they waited to be seated, heads turned. Stares from both women and men alike forced both women to fake a nonchalant attitude as if they got this much attention everyday. When asked what their seating preference was, Tiffenie said, "A corner table will be fine."

Once seated in a comfortable leather captain's chair, Thelma broke the silence with an abrupt, "Well Tiff, what's really goin' on?"

Sipping something delightful from a colorful straw, Tiffenie paused and said, "Well, Thelma, I like you very much, and it seems that we get along quite well, but..." She paused and took another sip of her drink.

"You don't know how it will be on the professional front to have a stripper for a friend," Thelma finished for her.

"Well yeah, at first I thought like that, but now I realize that very few, if any, care. It's not like I'm trying to judge you or anything. It's that I'm glad I have a friend."

Tiffenie took another sip of her drink and continued, "Look Thelma, I've practically been alone for the last three years since coming to this city. I had not realized how lonely I've been. When I called you the other day, I needed someone to talk to without judging me. Then I realized what I had been doing to you and other people was what people had done to me all of my life. Trying to control and punish folks just because they don't meet your standards which are not standards at all. Just judging other people out of their own fears. That's why I formally want you to be my best friend."

Even though her tone was light, Tiffenie was serious.

The two women raised their glasses and toasted. "Salute. Best friends for life, agreed?" Tiffenie asked.

"Agreed," Thelma responded.

She continued, "When I was in college, we giggled a lot and truly had some good times. I noticed when someone got into real trouble everybody got as far away from that person as possible. I remember that Harriet, a friend in our little circle, began acting strange. Instead of us getting involved and pressing her to tell us what was happening, we began to exclude her from our little events. Harriet committed suicide. She took an overdose of sleeping pills. I found out later that she was pregnant, by whom nobody knows. Her parents were Jehovah's Witnesses. I haven't felt right about myself since because of that incident. Thelma, if I or a couple of girls had gone to her and really pressed her as to what was going on, Harriet would be here today. It scares me to think of how many ways a person can die of loneliness."

Thelma sipped her rose-colored drink before looking directly at Tiffenie. "I've not told you much about me because there's not much to tell. I do what I do because minimum wage just don't get it. Believe me, it's a rush. It's a serious power rush to use my sexuality to control an audience. Yes, I enjoy that rush the way junkies enjoy their drugs. As far as men go, I haven't slept with a man in over a year and a half. I'm not gay or anything weird. I've just given up trusting anyone anymore. A woman, who I thought was my friend, did some serious damage that totally devastated me. I, like you, have been lonely so long it's become almost normal." She paused, taking another sip from her drink. "Let's end this drought of loneliness, Tiff. I'm going to take a chance on you." "Salute, Tiff."

"Salute, Thelma." They toasted and laughed.

Sandy, the bartender for that night, was so skilled at his trade that he could mix any drink without paying close attention. His hands flew that night for there were many customers. His practiced eye noticed the two women sitting at the far corner of the room.

The polished marble floor hosted the ebony and bronzed beauties. One ebony statue, in a thoughtful pose, turned

her profile eyes toward the ceiling, while the other
honey-toned beauty gazed deeply into her golden drink.

"Ready to go to the party?" Thelma asked, breaking the
solemn mood.

"Yeah, let's go," Tiffenie replied.

Once on the street, Thelma used a fashionable silver
whistle to summon a cab. The dark interior of the cab,
weaving its way through the traffic, gave the city lights
an aurora of mystery.

Tiffenie, in between laughs said, "Girl, you should of
seen him. He was dressed in a plaid suit with shoes so
pointed that you could pick your teeth with them. He
asked me what type of work I did. Girl, the nerve. I could
not believe it." Both women were holding their sides. The
laughter had become painful.

"417 Van Troupe Blvd., Mrs.," stated the cab driver.

"How did we get here so fast?" Thelma exclaimed.

"Shoot we came here in a helicopter," Tiffenie giggled to
Thelma. Again the women broke into gales of laughter.

"Girl, you is silly," stated Thelma.

"Naw, you the one," Tiffenie shot back.

On the sidewalk, the drum of many voices and blaring
music could be heard as the women entered the
brass-knobbed front door.

Thelma yelled over her shoulder, "I sure hope that you
can jump up, cause this is a Rhasta party."

Her words were snatched away by the many voices and
hues of people. The attire ranged from traditional African
garb to Ivy League, fancy shirt and jacket, and work
clothes. A dredlocked man pulled Tiffenie gently by the
arm onto the dance floor. At first, she had a difficult time
adjusting her body to the pulsating throb of the reggae
music, however, the liquor and reefer lent her body to the
beat. Before she knew it, she was jumping up, as Thelma

had called it. The DJ switched the music to a slower pace. The man she was dancing with pulled her to him. They began slow dancing. Looking over his shoulder, Tiffenie saw Thelma dancing with a man who seemed vaguely familiar. Thelma caught Tiffenie's eye and winked at her. After the record ended, Tiffenie thanked the man and joined Thelma in the lighted kitchen. The table was being used as the bar. People were standing around gabbing and gossiping.

"I haven't had this much fun for as long as I can remember," said Tiffenie.

"Me neither girl. I'm glad we came," Thelma answered. "Want me to fix you another drink?" Thelma asked.

"No, I've had enough," Tiffenie replied.

At that instant, a tall, dark man in a blue suit shoved a drink in her hand, and said, "Hello, fine lady. My name is Walter, what's yours?"

Tiffenie accepted the drink, suddenly becoming coy. She answered in a Shirley Temple voice. "Tiffenie," she said.

"Would you like to dance?"

"Not just yet," she replied.

"I've seen you before. I think downtown at the Lumpkin Building," he continued.

"Oh, now I remember you. That's where I have lunch sometimes. I don't work there. I work in the Pear Building. I'm a senior sales manager for Rosenthal Incorporated," she said with pride.

Walter, his complexion matching the hue of his black silk tie, cut a striking figure. His face, devoid of hair, gave him a youthful appearance. While Tiffenie was appraising his good looks, she caught him staring at Thelma over the top of her head.

"Oh dear, I seem to have a run in my stockings." Tiffenie turned to give Walter a bird's eye view of her rounded derrière.

"You come to the party with someone or by yourself?" he asked.

"I came with my friend, Thelma." She turned to introduce the two but Thelma had disappeared into the next room.

"She was here just a moment ago. I'll introduce you two later.

"Hey man. Walter, let me rap with you a minute," a man in dredlocks said, sticking his head around the kitchen corner.

"Yeah, I'll be right there." Turning to Tiffenie he said, "Be right back, Tiffenie." Before she could reply, he too disappeared into the swaying throng of humanity in the next room.

Thelma's eyes closed, at one with the music. The rhythm snatched and grabbed her body with each throb of the bass line. So engrossed with the subtle play between the music and her body, Thelma did not notice a group of men eyeing her intently. The guy that she was dancing with shuffled his feet in time with the music, mesmerized with her body. After the record ended, Thelma, with a start, discovered that she was attracting a lot of attention.

As she was heading for the kitchen, the man she had danced with grabbed her arm. "Hey baby, I got some hemp and some blow in my car. You want to ride?"

"Oh no, but I really enjoyed dancing with you," she replied, squirming out of his grasp.

In the kitchen, she found Tiffenie holding a conversation with a woman dressed in an African-American concept of traditional African garb.

"Are you a Pan-Africanist or a Nationalist?" Thelma heard her asking Tiffenie.

Tiffenie, lost for words, said, "Oh, I'm into Hands Across America."

The woman's facial expression broke into a incredulous stare. She said, "Sister, you can't be serious."

Thelma interrupted, "She's a Nationalist, but she is in a delicate developmental stage."

The woman threw her scarf across her shoulder and left the room, cutting her eyes in Tiffenie's direction. Thelma broke into a gale of laughter. Tiffenie, not sure of what she was laughing, at joined in.

"Girl friend, I thought you went to college. Didn't you get any political education?"

"Political education," Tiffenie repeated, knowing somehow that what Thelma was talking about did not come directly from the established school curriculum.

Before Tiffenie could go any further into the conversation, a man grabbed her hand and led her to the dance floor. Bouncing through the throng of bodies, he then turned to face her in the center of the room.

"Hey Tiffenie, remember me, I'm Jason."

He then pulled her to him. Tiffenie felt a warm flush envelope her body. She then leaned back holding his head between her hands and looked Jason directly in the eye.

"Yeah, I remember you. You're the guard who works in my building."

Jason laughed softly and held her closer. Tiffenie relinquished and merged her body close to his, resting her head on his shoulder.

"I'm surprised to see you at this type of party," he said.

"I don't know why you would be surprised to see me here, you don't even know me," Tiffenie replied.

"I know enough about you to know that I think I like you very much."

"Now how can you not know me and still like me?" she asked.

"I said that I might *think* I might like you," he countered.

At a lost for what to say, and becoming increasingly intoxicated by one another's nearness and scent, they danced through two torrid slow records without saying a word.

Thelma found a seat on the couch which gave her a ring side view of the dancing couples. She smiled as she watched the hips of Tiffenie and Jason undulate suggestively against each other. She leaned back into the comfort of the couch, wallowing in its comfort.

Thelma had almost dozed off when a man shoved her shoulder and said, "Hey Sparkel, what's up"?

On hearing one of her old stage names, Thelma's tranquil expression turned into a cold, glittering stare. "I'm tired that's what's up," she replied, hoping that he would feel the vibes and leave.

"Don't play that brush off shit with me, woman. I know where you work," he stated. Contempt sharpened his tongue.

"Well, if you so upset of what I do, why don't you quit annoying me and take your tired conked head home to your wife," she shot back.

Jason felt Tiffenie's succulent body become ridged next to him. "What's wrong," he asked.

They turned simultaneously to see a man standing over Thelma shouting, "I don't know how a slut like you got into a party like this anyway."

Thelma jumped up, snatching her purse. The man grabbed her arm, slinging her back onto the couch.

Before anyone had an idea of what was taking place, they saw another woman come streaking off the dance area, hurtling her form at the man screaming, "I'm going to kill you, talking to us like that!" Tiffenie began plummeting him with her fists. The man shoved her to the floor. In a motion, Tiffenie picked up a lamp and threw it at the man. The large globe shattered against the corner table. With a back hand, the man knocked Tiffenie to the floor.

Thelma had recovered. She got a running start and jumped on the man's back. With her legs wrapped around his waist, she maliciously clawed his face. They tumbled to the couch. Jason joined in the melee, attempting to separate the grappling figures. Tiffenie was attempting with all of her pent up rage to scratch the man's eyes out. All four bodies tumbled from the couch to the floor.

The host of the party, a man of dubious means and popular in general, stood in shock like the rest of his guests.

"Everybody, help me separate them," he shouted. The crowd of onlookers converged on the frantic group and eventually, with superior numbers, halted the disturbance.

Tiffenie and Thelma were taken screaming into the kitchen, while the men were left standing in the livingroom. Jason's left eye had begun to swell. He stood with both arms pinned behind his back. He faced the man who had initiated the free for all, who was held also.

"What the fuck is yo' problem, man, starting shit like that," said Jason heatedly.

The man called Low Down answered, "Fuck you, mutha and both dem bitches. Y'all going to pay, scratching up my face like this. Let me go." He stormed out the front door, knocking over a lamp in the process.

Jomo had come to the scene late. He had been out taking care of a little business. Jomo had thought the scene extremely amusing and had at first enjoyed what he called a bit of drama — until he realized who the man was. He followed Jason into the kitchen to see about the girls.

J ason found Tiffenie and Thelma looking like they just got off a runaway L train. Their stockings were torn, tear-stained makeup made rivets of uneven streaks down their faces. Both women were sniffling.

Tiffenie's cleaving silk dress had all but given up covering her breasts. Jason took off his jacket and draped it over her shoulders. Tiffenie looked up, thanking him with her eyes. Thelma was staring off into space as if she was not a part of this set. There was a bruise under her left eye that had begun to swell.

"That might need some medical attention," Jomo stated, looking closely at Thelma's face. "You OK?" he asked, concern registering in his voice.

Thelma sighed loudly and nodded her head. "I'm just sorry I came, and I'm real sorry that I got you involved, Tiff."

Tiffenie hugged Thelma to her, "We ain't even goin' to go there ,girlfriend. We in this to the end." Both women began sobbing anew.

Jason stood and said, "Look, we'll take you two home. There is the bathroom. Y'all go on and get cleaned up."

Jomo, lowering his voice, said, "Low Down ain't as funny as he looks. This shit ain't over."

"Yeah, I know," replied Jason.

The host of the party could be heard saying good night to the remaining guests. Ralph entered the lighted kitchen and asked, "Are the girls all right?"

"They straight. A little bruised up, but they be all right," Jomo replied.

"As soon as they come out of the bathroom, we're goin' to take them home. Sorry about the damage to your furniture and the disturbance," Jason said.

Jomo handed Ralph a wad of money. Ralph thumbed through it and gave most of it back.

"These things happen and the damage is not as bad as it looks. I just hope y'all resolve something with Low Down. I'm tired of us Brothers killing Brothers, no matter what the reason."

Thelma turned the corner followed by Tiffenie. "We ready, Jason. Me and Thelma live close, so you won't have to go so far out of the way."

"Yeah, we goin' to take y'all home but we're going in my car. The back seat of that Camero just don't get it," Jomo stated.

Slowing at a stop light, Jomo turned to Thelma, staring out of the window in the front seat. "East Side or West Side?"

"West side, Jomo, and take the beltway, it will be quicker," Thelma answered.

"You from around here?" Jomo asked.

"Naw, I'm from Kansas," she answered.

The car fell silent. Jason and Tiffenie were snuggled up in the back seat like high school lovers. Jomo observed them in his rearview mirror and smiled.

The large, late model Oldsmobile 98 pulled silently up to the curb in front of Thelma's apartment building, "How about letting me take you to a movie or something," Jomo asked, as he escorted her to the front door.

Thelma paused. "I don't know, Jomo, I haven't dated in a while," her voice trailed off.

"This ain't no rush thing. Just take your time. I'll be around. Is that a bet?"

"Call me Sunday, late in the day, Tiff has my number."

After dropping Tiffenie off, Jomo headed back across town to drop Jason off at his car.

"Man, we sho' ran into some fine honeys tonight," Jomo exclaimed.

"Got that right, Jomo. What are we going to do about Low Down?"

"I'm a goin' to try to talk to that crazy mutha tomorrow. I know somebody that he supplies. If that ain't no deal, we got problems, Jason. That nigga is crazy. Plus, he's connected. Yeah, he is a criminal in the true sense of the word."

"Shit. Find somethin' good and there it is, somethin' fucked up right in the middle," Jason stated.

Jason made a U-turn, and shouted out of his open window, "Tomorrow, Jomo."

When Thelma climbed into bed, she thought that she would have a difficult time getting to sleep. She awoke with sunshine streaming through her flat. Sitting up, she groaned from the soreness in her back and thighs. "Whew, that was some night," she said aloud. Suddenly, like a cloud, her head dropped, the man had made her feel ashamed of herself. What else could she do?

She thought about returning to night school to be a secretary. Suddenly, she laughed. She did not want to do any of that shit. The reality of it was that Thelma enjoyed what she did. What was wrong with that? It all came down to money, and that was not funny.

The jangling of her phone caused her to jump.

"Thelma, you up?" Tiffenie's voice come across the line.

"Yeah, I just woke up. How you feel?"

"Like I've been playin' football with Reggie White," Tiffenie answered.

"Me too, girlfriend, and I thought that dancing kept me in shape."

"What are you going to do today, Thelma?"

"Sleep and eat, lay around and watch television. That's what I do every Sunday," she explained.

"Let's go to church. I haven't been in ages and there is an old Baptist church just across town."

Thelma paused, then said, "If you don't start a fight."

Both women broke out into gales of laughter.

"See you in a hour," Tiffenie said before hanging up.

"We are the soldiers in the army. We got to fight, although we have to die." The chords came floating out of the church doors. Thelma was singing softly along.

"I can tell you ain't nothing but a old church girl," Tiffenie commented.

Thelma smiled and continued to sing along softly.

Midsummer had brought, with its heavy, damp morning breeze, the aroma of birch and evergreen trees. The church was located in the middle of a long block, allowing the women the luxury of an unhurried Sunday morning walk. Thelma, dressed in a blue frock and Tiffenie in a white summer dress, were quite a contrast to the way they were dressed last Thursday night.

Just inside the great oak doors, matronly women clad in sober white ushered them to a side room. A silver-haired elder said, "Sorry, you can't go in just yet. The Wheelbarrow Choir is opening the services. After the first song a stocky Sister dressed in gleaming white escorted them to their seats.

Thelma glanced around her — she had come from this fold. Uniformed women stationed at intervals along the blood red carpet aisles, brought back fond memories. It was her grandmother who had brought her to church every Sunday without fail. A sense of warmth and belonging invaded her entire being.

The choir rendition of *"We are the soldiers"* ended, and a coal black, razor thin man entered the pulpit. The flowing black robe swished to a halt as his hawklike gaze swept the audience.

"Brothers and Sisters, we are in troubled times." The audience agreed with nods of their heads and low moans of amens.

"These are the times when the old bury the young and the future is cloudy before the most wisest of the learned men." He paused and swept the audience again with his penetrating gaze.

"These are times when the grey clouds of injustice and confusion run rampant over this land. We see fathers and mothers abandon their children. We see children commit horrendous crimes. For us, there is no option. We must turn to our savior and lord, Jesus Christ. Let us bow our heads and pray."

He stepped to the front of the pulpit, stretched out his arms as if he were going to fly, and said, "let us bow our heads."

Thelma glanced at Tiffenie, she smiled and bowed her head.

The preacher continued, "Dear God, bless these children when they're lonely. Give us, as Black people, the strength to solve the problems that besiege us. Forgive the drug addicts as well as the dealers. Forgive the women gone astray. Give peace and condolence to the many young Black men crowding this country's prisons. Most importantly, dear Lord, let our children know that it is their duty, if they are more fortunate, to reach back and help their Brothers or Sisters along. It is their duty as Africans and Christians to reach out, even if it's inconvenient, to help all of their people move forward."

With a concise motion of his arm, the choir began their rendition of 'Peace Be Still'.

A stillness pervaded the packed church. The multicolored windows altered the sun's rays to a purple hue. Thelma, singing softly, lost herself in the words, peace be still.

Just before leaving the protective oak doors, the silver-haired elder, who had let them in, whispered to Thelma, "Don't leave before I talk to you both."

At the conclusion of the service, everyone stood around in the anteroom smiling and congratulating each other. Tiffenie noticed that Thelma had a radiant glow about her. The stout woman, who had seated them at the beginning of the service, motioned for Thelma and Tiffenie to follow her. She led them to a cluttered office where the silver-haired elder was seated behind an equally cluttered desk.

"Hello, to you both. I'm Sister Clarice," she stated, rising from her desk to shake both of their hands. "Have a seat."

Seated in a straight-backed chair facing the desk, Tiffenie crossed her legs and looked around the room. In the far corner was a picture of Jesus. He was wooly headed and bronze skinned and surrounded by sheep on a hillside.

"It's good to see fine young women like yourselves come to worship with us this bright and sunny Sunday." She turned her attention to Thelma, who for some reason, could not look her in the eye.

"So Thelma, where are you from?" she asked point blank.

"Kansas," Thelma replied.

"Well, go on and tell me a little about yourself. My intention is not to pry or get into your personal business. We need young people like yourselves to give us a new perspective and new ideas," Sister Clarice stated firmly. She paused and stated, "You might even have some need for us."

"Well, I'm not married, and I just started getting out again a couple of days ago. I really enjoyed your service. It reminded me when I was a little girl and used to go to church with my grandmother." Thelma's voice trailed off into silence.

Sister Clarice turned her attention to Tiffenie, who had noticed that Thelma had gone to some distant train of

thought that left others out. Thelma's distant stare reminded Tiffenie of the other night when they had been
involved in the big fight.

"Oh, me," Tiffenie caught herself. "Well, I work at the
Pear Building as a senior manager. I'm not married either. I don't have a steady man right now, but I just met
someone that seems nice and we seem compatible. Me and
Thelma have recently become best friends. We sort of
saved each other," she added as an afterthought." Tiffenie
looked Thelma in the eye and Thelma returned her open
stare.

"Should I tell her, or will you?" Thelma asked, coming
out of her trance.

"I will," Tiffenie volunteered. "It's some things that I
haven't told you," she began.

"Like what, Tiff?" Thelma asked.

Tiffenie drew a deep breath and straightened her pos-
ture.

"I was shopping in Krocer's. That particular day, I was
extremely depressed and irritable. While at the vegetable
counter, I grabbed the same head of cabbage that Thelma
had grabbed. We caused such a row. Can you imagine two
grown women arguing over a head of cabbage? I snatched
the cabbage head from her and threw it down the isle. She
looked at me and shook her head and laughed." She
glanced in Thelma's direction and smiled. "Well," she
continued, still smiling, "The most surprising statement
came out of her mouth. She said, 'It's been that rough, has
it?' Then she offered me a drink at her apartment." She
paused, a thoughtful expression crossed her face. She
continued, "What I never have revealed to Thelma is that,
at that time in my life, I was seriously contemplating
suicide."

Thelma's eyes widened, but she remained silent.

Sister Clarice leaned back in her chair, allowing the silence to settle. Finally, she said, "Well, I hope you girls come back to see us again. Here is my phone number. I insist that you give me a call from time to time".

Thelma thought Sister Clarice out of place.

The morning's sun had rolled around to its noon position by the time the two women were walking back to their apartments. They took their time, taking in the scenery and people.

"That was nice, real nice," Tiffenie said.

"Yeah, that was," Thelma agreed. "You know what?"

"What," Tiffenie replied.

"I don't know exactly what I want out of life, but I am going to take my time and find out," Thelma said. She continued, "Tiff, I have really enjoyed myself these last couple of days. That self isolation stuff just don't get it. Nobody should have to live like that. I mean, you can't be fair to yourself. Know what I mean?"

"Don't I," agreed Tiffenie.

"I can still remember the kind of perfume that my grandmother used. Sister Clarice uses the same brand. That scent. It freaked me out. Memories, girl, memories," Thelma repeated shaking her head. "How do you think you and Jason are going to make out?"

"I'm very comfortable with him. Like I'm not looking for him to pull out a hatchet on the first date. At least he don't seem c-r-a-z-y. He might even have the sensitivity that I need in a relationship. Bottom line girl, I haven't had any in ages."

Both women broke into giggles.

"What about that Rhasta guy Jomo, Jason's partner. What you think y'all going to do? Tiffenie asked.

"I really don't know. Lord knows that I need to be with someone. But, I ain't about to go through hell and back for no orgasm," she replied ruefully. "It would be nice if we could begin as friends."

Climbing her front stairs, Thelma glanced at a golden red sun ending the day. The sound of her phone ringing made her think of heavy dredlocks. She did not see the ancient, yellow Cadillac rolling silently pass her stoop.

"**Y**o L-oo-w Down, what up mon?" a cinnamon-hued man asked from the street. He was wearing a heavy gold chain and a sparkling pair of tennis shoes. He walked up to the yellow Caddy from the street side.

"What up, baby boy," Low Down answered, turning his head toward the street.

"What the fuck happened to you?" Chuck asked, shocked at the deeply etched scratches and bruises on Low Down's face.

"I got into some shit. It's goin' to be taken care of. You want something, muthafucka, or you just concerned about my welfare? Low Down responded, ghetto hostile style.

"Yeah, I need a ounce and a half. I need it right away, if you holdin'," Chuck replied, apprehensive about dealing with Low Down when he was in a bad mood.

"Meet me at the house in about twenty minutes." Chuck turned to leave. "Oh yeah, Chuck, tell Scoot that I want him and a couple of his boys to meet me there too."

"You got it," Chuck replied.

Low Down owned one of the few houses in the Neil Town district that wasn't public-housing. The largest project was only a couple of blocks from his. This made it convenient for his line of business. Not only was he one of the major distributors of cocaine, but he dealt in stolen goods, ranging from hot cars, to microwave ovens.

Most of the men that he dealt with, he had grown up with or had met in prison. He was a very hard man to get to unless he wanted you to. Despite his rough shod appearance, he was a good business man and made a lot of people a lot of money. The uptown boys with all the loose change invested lucratively with him. The perks afforded him were numerous. He could get political favors from reducing a prison sentence to getting the police to bungle an investigation, even for murder.

Jomo understood this and prepared for the worst possible events as he tied on his bullet proof vest and stuck his 9mm into his waist band.

"Yo Jack, let me talk to you," Jomo said, as a heavy-set man was admonishing a stacked young lady in one of the many narrow openings that ran through the projects.

The woman, dressed in biker shorts and a loose tee-shirt, was obviously upset, gesturing wildly. She tried to walk away, but Jack grabbed her arm and positioned her back in front of him.

"Bitch, if you ever bring somebody like that to my spot again, I'm goin' to break your back."

"He seemed cool to me, besides you didn't turn down his money, muthafucka. Give it up," she demanded.

He reached into his jeans pocket and handed her three hard, white rocks. She palmed them and proceeded down the narrow walkway, throwing her hips provocatively from side to side.

"Fuck you, Jack," she yelled, when she was a safe distance from him.

Jack laughed and shook his head. He headed for Jomo, who was still seated in his car. He leaned into Jomo's car from the driver side. "Yeah, what's up, Jomo?"

"I need to talk to Low Down," Jomo stated. Before he could explain further, Jack interrupted.

"Yeah, yeah, man. I was at the party and Low Down was wrong, but, if I was you, I'd let that shit ride and stay as far away from them bitches as you can, 'cause Low Down goin' to do somethin' to both them hoes."

Jomo looked in his rear view mirror and said, "Just tell Low Down that I want to talk to him."

"I'll do that because it's you, Jomo, but all it's going to do is make matters worse. That was some funny shit, though them bitches fucked Ol' Boy up."

Jack walked away from the car, looking back over his shoulder, laughing and shaking his head.

Nigga think everything so funny, thought Jomo, as he speed away from the curb.

Low Down sat in a low, overstuffed couch. He neither smiled nor frowned. Seated before him, were Scoot, Turtle and Little Mack.

"This is the deal. There are some young bloods that are trying to take over my reefer business on the West Side. I want them muthas hit," Low Down stated.

Little Mack's name was deceiving — he was anything but small of statue. The name Little Mack was bestowed upon him because his hands were so big. A Mack Ten submachine gun looked like a toy in his huge hands.

Scoot sat idle looking out of the huge bay window, while Turtle constantly fidgeted running his hands over his processed hair as he chain smoked Lucky Strikes cigarettes.

"Look, Low Down, the hit on the young boys is legit, but I ain't about to take a chance on wasting some stupid strip dancer because she ripped up your face. Let's beat the fuck out of her and the other bitch and let it go at that. Besides, all hits have to be OK'd by the Board, and you and I know that they ain't even thinking about no bullshit like this," Scoot stated evenly.

"What you two think?" Low Down asked the other seated guests.

"I don't give a fuck who I hit, just as long as the money is right," Turtle replied.

"I say let's just fuck up the bitches, get some of that pussy and call it a day. But to kill two bitches, just ain't my style," said Little Mack.

There was a knock on the door. Low Down excused himself to answer it. It was Jack. He entered and greeted the men with, "What's up, little confused bitches?"

No one returned greetings with Jack. They just watched him without a flicker of emotion.

"Jack is here because Jomo wants to set up a meeting so that we can resolve this matter of these bitches scratching up my face in front of all those people," Low Down stated. Sarcasm dripping from each word.

"I knew that it would not do any good, but Jomo is a friend of mine and I promised him that I would deliver the message. You know that Jason and him are partners."

"Is that the muthafucka that jumped into the fight?" Low Down asked.

"Yeah, that's him," Jack answered.

"Well, tell Jomo, fuck him and don't even think about it."

"Well, I did deliver the message," Jack said.

"What you want for it, a Tootsie Roll?" Mack said.

"Naw, I just wanted to see four little bitches sitting around a table trying to figure out what hair style they gone to wear for the big dance."

"Get gone, muthafucka," Low Down stated, raising a pistol from beneath the table.

"I'm outta here, boss," Jack replied, backing out the door, shaking his head and smiling.

"That muthafucka think everything is so funny," said Turtle.

"If he keep on talkin' crazy to me, he gone to find out ain't nuthin' as funny as he think, and I bet that shit," Low Down muttered under his breath.

There was a knock on the door. Low Down got up to answer it. "Who is it?" he asked through the closed door.

"It's me Silvia."

A brown-skinned women entered, dressed in a downtown business suit.

"Here, I brought you the statements," she said, digging into a leather attache case. It was very expensively made of soft, flexible leather.

"Thank you, Silvia. Is there anything that I can get for you?" he asked.

"Oh no, I'm on my way back downtown. I have another meeting in about an hour."

She left the same way that she had entered, all business.

"Who dat?" Turtle asked.

"None of your business, and, if you even see her on the street, don't even act like you know her," Low Down said.

"Oh, I guess dat bitch better then me," Turtle replied.

"Yeah, she better then you and she show nuff business and essential to our enterprises."

"Enterprises, essential — shit nigga where you get that language?" Turtle asked, laughing.

Low Down ignored the remark and said, "OK, my niggas, time for y'all to earn yo money. Remember when you do dem young niggas that's tryin' to take over our reefer business, let their bodies be found. It will be an example for the rest of them that think that they can take anything from Low Down."

After the men had left, he turned to open his curtains. The street was empty this time of the day. He remembered when he was a snotty-nosed kid running errands for who he thought were the neighborhood bigshots. A lot of

people that he did business with asked him why he stayed
here. He always told them that he liked to be close to his
action. Always, he knew that it was the memory of his
mother that kept him here.

His real name was Jimmy Lane. He thought of his
mother dying from diabetes in their run down tenement
apartment. His blood ran cold with the thought of what
happened to her. She was one of the few people who really
cared about him. Sometimes he felt that he had come a
long way. Other times he felt that he was still that runny
nosed kid that nobody living really cared about. His career began when the local crime lord got gunned down by
a rival faction. At seventeen, Low Down had no concept of
fear. He had offed the three other rival crime lords himself. Then he emerged as the number one crime boss of
that particular district. It was his downtown connections
that made him powerful. Now he controlled all but a
corner of the North Side district. He sat in his easy chair
and closed his eyes.

The afternoon sun began its downward plunge. Shadows
splashed themselves haphazardly between looming tenement buildings. The daytime inhabitants scurried toward
established places of comfort. The nighttime inhabitants
greeted the night with anticipation.

Aspotlight wove its way through the darkened throng. A faint cadence palpitated its way into the multitude's ears, causing feet to involuntarily tap with the beat. The drummer and the bass player of this particular tune were exchanging rhythms while the disc jockey slowly raised the volume. Colors burst from the spotlight, giving the room and its populace a greenish glow. Silence settled. The hushed onlookers' anticipation was about to be satiated. Thelma, the dancer, had high-stepped out. With each step, her legs lifted higher. She stood center stage with the spotlight draped around her. She swayed gently like a tree in the breeze. Then, in the middle of the rhythm, she snapped her hips and thighs to the downdrop of a heavy rap beat. Thelma reached, deep flexing and slinging her hips to every alternate rimshot. She stood in one spot and gyrated, a puddle of sweat forming on the floor. The sea of upturned heads bobbed to the beat. They began to clap, joining in the performance. Her short, tightly-curled, glistening hair fit like a skullcap. It lay plastered to her brown, perspiring face. Her breasts fit snugly against her knit halter. Globe-shaped hips bounced and quivered with every synchronized movement.

Reaching toward the ceiling, Thelma moonwalked in slow motion across the stage. She signaled the disc jockey to pick up the tempo. Cavorting, bumping and grinding a loose version of the fan dance, she let it all hang out. Elbows, arms, hips, and thighs gyrating to a unknown inner rhythm. The audience was cast spellbound. Wait-

resses no longer served the customers. They had suc-
cumbed to the spell that Thelma had cast.

Thelma spun on her heels and walked off stage, jarring
her body into her acclaimed catwalk. There was a pause,
then a thunderous round of applause from the audience. A
couple on the front row stood and applauded, raising their
hands encouraging the throng of humanity to stand clap-
ping into a frenzy.

While standing off stage, Thelma's eyes reflected a distant ambience. Waves and waves of applause, hoots, and
catcalls rebounded off the night club walls. The sounds
followed her into the depths of the building, into her
dressing room.

Thelma sat in front of her dressing room mirror, trying
to find nonexistent wrinkles. Left alone at last, Thelma
changed into her street clothes, baggy jeans and a sweat
shirt. She swung her bag onto her shoulder as there was a
knock on the door. This one even and hard.

"Yes, come in," she answered.

"You decent?" a man's voice asked.

"I said come in, didn't I?" her tone curt.

A large man entered. He was dressed in a brown silk
suit, white shirt and matching silk tie. He pulled out the
overused, brown chair from the corner of the room and
settled his large frame comfortably in it.

"Well, don't mind me Boone, just make yourself comfortable," she stated, sarcasm in her voice.

"And what do I get for my troubles — a smart ass
women that needs to listen to somebody sometime."

"OK. It's late. What do you want, Boone?"

"I got a deal that will satisfy us both," he began.

"Oh, you're going to commit suicide," she quipped.

"Look bitch, let's cut the fun and games. You owe our
people money. You got a skill that's making this dead-end

joint a lot of money. The Big Boys want you to dance at the Fox Room across town. You dance for him, your debt is automatically paid and you'll be well compensated for your work. Don't get cute, Thelma. I'm not above knockin' the shit out of you, just for good ol' times sake," he stated coolly leaning forward.

Thelma noted the glint in Boone's eyes. She knew that he would do that and much more.

"I'm cool, Boone, I just don't like the idea of everybody trying to muscle me."

She paused and rummaged in her bag for an ill-rolled joint. Thelma lit it and took a drag, blowing the smoke at the ceiling.

"Look Boone, thanks but no thanks. I got some type of control of my act here and I ain't into having sex for money or doing lesbian scenes on stage with other women. Besides, I'll have my debts paid off by the end of next month."

"Look Thelma I'll be straight with you, Striker don't want to loose you and he don't intend to. You're in demand. Some very influential people saw you last night and they been asking around about you. Those uptown guys..." his voice trailed off.

"What does Striker want out of me? I'm going to give him his money."

"Striker wants control of everything that can make him money, Thelma. He figures you don't have no protection and he can get his way with controlling you since you still owe him three thousand seven hundred and forty five dollars."

"You're not telling me this out of the goodness of your heart, Boone. If Striker knew that you come to me with another deal with his competitors, he'd have your carcass swimming in the bay."

Thelma's antenna was up — something was fishy.

Boone spread his hands in front of him as if he was about to play a piano. "Look Thelma, I got plans. I got connects out west and Atlanta. I can hook up you and two other girls, and we can make a run for the border. Look at your options. You got Low Down breathing down your neck, you owe Striker money, and the uptown boys want you. And I know you've heard about Mr. Raymore," he paused, then continued.

"Well... I sort of like you, Thelma. You a nice girl. You wouldn't have to dance for long. You could just keep the books and handle the business," his voice trailed off.

Thelma almost fell from her chair. "I didn't know that you had it in you, Boone. I appreciate the offer, but no way, José. I know that you liked Susan and I know what happened to her." She paused, her eyebrow arched. "Yeah, the police fished her out of the river. If I did leave with you, what do you have on Striker that would keep him from coming after you?"

He rose abruptly, "Well that's the best offer that you going to get. I give you credit, you ain't no stupid bitch. Things are about to change in this part of the woods. If I was you, I wouldn't want to be part of the shrubbery.

"You didn't answer my question, Boone."

"I know," he replied, closing the door softly behind him.

The subway ride home was lost on the lights and glitter of the city.

Thelma's apartment was located at the very top of the staircase. Unlike the rest of the complex, it was white-washed in a glimmering variety of white shades. The wooden trim was painted a gray white color while the walls a shimmering white gloss. The hardwood floors were decorated with a tasteful array of Chinese and Per-

sian throw rugs. Thelma had purchased these items
through the city's black market trade. The quality was
the best money could buy.

She threw herself in one of her oversized, padded wicker
chairs.

"Whew, what a day, what a day," she exclaimed loudly to
herself. Reaching under the coffee table, she extracted a
lighter and a crumpled pack of cigarettes.

Blowing smoke toward the ceiling, she stretched with
upturned hands straining upward. At the point where
stretching is most pleasurable, a hurried knock sounded
at the door, bringing her to a standing position.

"Yes?" Thelma said, facing the door.

"It's me, Tiff."

Laughing, Thelma swung open the door, turned her back
to her visitor and said, "Come on in, girlfriend. I just got
in."

"Did you knock 'em dead?"

Thelma turned with a mock mean stare, balled fist on
her perfect hips, left foot forward demonstrating her
buffalo stance. "You know them men lost their minds,
soul, and money."

With that, she snatched up her shoulder bag. Reaching
in, she extracted a small paper sack. She flipped the
parcel to the ceiling. On impact, it erupted into hundreds
of fluttering one and five dollar bills.

Tiffenie threw back her mahogany head and laughed.

"I'll have to get up enough nerve to come and catch one
of your shows," Tiffenie stated. She stared with admiration and awe at her friend.

Thelma's cat eyes narrowed while flashing a glittering
stare. She answered, "Monday night's the best. Hey, it's
nothing but a dollar." Her voice betrayed a defensiveness
that was not lost on Tiffenie.

"Just stopped by to say hi, I'm off to work. I'll call you when I think you're awake."

Thelma closed the door behind Tiffenie and began to get ready for bed.

The sun rays rose high in the early Autumn sky.

Beads of sweat slowly rolled from beneath his chin. The man, crouched in the alley, shifted his weight from one foot to another. He rose slightly to peer intently at a grey metal door. The man had positioned himself behind a large green dumpster that faced that door.

The man tensed, the grey door swung open. He donned a bright red ski mask, then pulled a large automatic pistol from his waist. He moved quickly towards the guards that were transporting the cash for the largest payroll office in the city. G & W Power & Light Company, the letters read on the black and gold armored car. Sully, as he was called by his friends, was jolted wide awake as he looked into the enormous gun barrel that was pointed directly between his eyes.

Ron, his partner, had not an inkling of what was going on. He was inside the armored car waiting for Sully to start handing him the money.

"Hey Ron, you'd better get out here," Sully stated flatly.

"What the hell is it now?" Ron asked, sticking his head out of the truck window. Ron froze, looking down at the masked man.

"Get the fuck out of the van and lay on the ground," the masked figure growled.

The robber had a sturdy plastic bag which he stuffed most of the money into. He then coolly pointed the heavy pistol at the temple of the first guard's head and pulled the trigger. The second guard vainly tried to roll away while grabbing for his weapon. Two shots rent the still morning air. One bullet tore a gaping hole in his chest.

The other ripped into his stomach. His body flopped like a fish in the bottom of a boat then lay quiet.

The robber walked briskly to the next alley and disappeared into its hollowness.

It was still quite early for the business section of the city. It was almost twenty minutes after the robbery and the double murder had taken place before someone spotted the bazaar scene in the alley and called the police.

Shrill sirens filled the air.

Tiffenie looked up. The sirens were close, just down the street. She stood and looked out of her office window. Vehicles of all types belonging to the city's police department were speeding down the side street that her office window overlooked.

Returning to her desk, Tiffenie began humming to herself. She flipped through the countless row of numbers displayed on her computer. Lowering her lips to her intercom, she said, "Oh Mrs. Pitney, tell Mr. Michaels that I'm ready for those figures from last week's sale."

"Right away," Mrs. Pitney replied.

Tiffenie felt surprisingly refreshed for a Monday morning. A soft knock sounded on her office door.

"Come in," she responded. Mr. Rosenthal in a dark blue suit, entered with a folder in his hand.

"Oh Mr. Rosenthal, I thought you were Mr. Michaels bringing me the figures from last week."

Rosenthal, his hand resting on the door knob, replied, "I was in the accounting office when you called. I thought I'd bring the figures up myself." He handed Tiffenie the folder and hesitated.

Tiffenie waited. She had expected him to leave.

"Have a seat, Jim," she froze on a smile.

The collar on his starched shirt was pinching his red neck into a thin white line of flesh. Once seated, he began,

"I just stopped by to make sure that you're comfortable with the setup around here and to tell you about our annual Goose Sale Dinner. The company expects all of our senior managers and sales personnel to attend." The last sentence was stated flatly.

"When is it?" She asked, stalling for time. She had known about it for the last month.

"It's this Friday night, Tiffenie. We'll expect you about nine-thirty." Rosenthal stated.

The tone in his voice made Tiffenie wary. "I'll be there at nine-thirty. What shall I tell my date to wear?" she asked demurely.

At the mention of a date, Rosenthal lost some of his authoritative assurance. "A regular business suit will do." He paused. "I know that some of you around here think that I'm stuck up and a killjoy. I really ain't nuthin' but a good ol' farm boy. Down to earth, know what I mean?" he asked Tiffenie, eyeing her closely.

Tiffenie stood up and leaned toward the man seated on the other side of her desk. "I did not get the impression that you were stuck-up, Jim. In fact, you remind me of a farmer I once knew."

Rosenthal, caught off guard, hastily said, "Well, we'll see you at the party. Got to get some of this work done." He hurried out of the office.

As soon as the door closed, Tiffenie suppressed a giggle with her hand over her mouth.

Returning from lunch, Tiffenie's carefree mood changed into worry. Jason had not called her this weekend nor had he called her at the office. She was not sure what time he got to work, but he was usually there when she worked overtime. Tiffenie looked up the number for the front lobby security desk. She did not want to seem desperate

— after all he was only a security guard. She lost herself in the endless row of numbers on the screen of her computer and decided not too call him.

As she was getting off the elevator, Tiffenie planned to walk past the security desk slowly. If he did not speak, she would just walk out. Her plans were thwarted, because, standing next to the main door, was Jason talking to another Black woman. Tiffenie recognized her from the word processing department. She mentally processed every item that the woman wore: her shoes, stockings, makeup, dress, and accessories.

Jason noticed her watching them, then excused himself and walked over. "Hey, how are you doing?" he asked.

Tiffenie turned toward him, bringing her lips inches from his. "What's wrong, your finger broke?" she asked, trying to mask her unexpected anger.

"Look, I'm sorry that I didn't call, but I wasn't sure if you wanted me to," Jason answered, his eyebrows arched.

Tiffenie leaned closer. "Nigga, I gave you my home and office number. Something I haven't given any man in a long time. Now are you going to call me or not?"

"Yes, I'll call you as soon as you get home," he answered smiling.

"You'd better," she stated with mock ferocity. Surprising herself as well as Jason, she glared at the woman he'd been talking to as she left through the revolving glass doors.

Tiffenie had just gotten out of her dress and fixed herself a hot toddy, when the phone rang. "Hello," she answered.

"Hey Tiffenie, this is Jason." There was a long pause.

"Well, it's about time you called. Look Jason, if you don't want to see me, just say so, but don't have me thinking something that ain't happening," Tiffenie said.

Jason laughed softly, "I want to get to know you, Tiffenie, and I like you a lot, but I'm just a security guard." There was another long pause.

"It don't mean that we're going to get married. It just means we'll reach some type of understanding." She waited.

Jason said, "I got to go now. How about me stopping by tonight when I get off, about eleven thirty?"

"OK Jason, but don't come too late. I have to get up early to go to work, you know," Tiffenie answered.

Tiffenie took a brief nap then began cooking something for a late night snack. An impish grin appeared on her face. Tiffenie had an outfit that she had bought last month at a lingerie show. "Wonder if Jason will like this," she said aloud to herself.

Jason, not knowing what to expect, rang the buzzer to Tiffenie's apartment. She answered the door dressed in a purple satin pajama outfit. Her perfume assailed his nostrils. The effect went straight to his sexual organ. He hoped that she would not notice his erection.

"Come on into the kitchen, I fixed a little something for you to munch on."

Jason followed her ample hips into the kitchen, wondering if he could munch on something besides food.

Once seated at the table, Jason said, "Look Tiffenie, I came to talk to you about how I feel and where this relationship can go. I'm not nothing to play with. If you're full of games, I ain't the one."

"No Jason, I'm through with games. Games are for people who don't know what they want out of life. I want something real. Now, whether or not we have a long term relationship or a short one, I want it to be real. Forget living for someone else's ideas. I want to live."

Tiffenie's intensity astonished Jason.

"What do you want from me, Tiffenie? It's like I'm scared to get involved, because I just don't want to get hurt. I'm crazy enough as it is."

"That night at the party, you made me feel alive. I even enjoyed the fight we had with that sorry piece of shit. I've been stuck up in a corporate jail." She paused and watched him take a bite of chicken. "Jason I'm going to live life to its fullest. That doesn't mean that I'm going to do something negative or detrimental. I not going to let anybody use me, nor am I a user."

"Got any beer?" Jason asked, covering his mouth with his hand.

"No, I don't have any beer, but I have some wine. After you're finished, we'll go out into the front room and I'll serve it there," Tiffenie answered.

"That was a good meal, Tiffenie. Which way is the little boys room?"

"Down the hall and to the right," she answered.

Jason emerged from the bathroom and reclined on a black velvet love couch. He could hear Tiffenie in the kitchen breaking the ice free. She brought out a tray with an ice container and some glasses. She sat across from him in a matching chair.

"Well, Jason tell me about you," Tiffenie said.

Jason, with a full stomach and a conducive environment, relaxed and told her about his experiences in the war, his parents and his attempts to make more money. Tiffenie's attentive gaze made him forget about the time and, before either of them knew it, the clock read a quarter past two in the morning.

Jason reluctantly rose, stretching, "Well it's about time that I push away from here. Thanks for the dinner and company. I really enjoyed myself," he stated.

Tiffenie escorting him to the door realized how tired she was, muffled a yawn. "Jason are we going to continue seeing one another?"

"Hell yeah, Tiffenie. I haven't felt this way, ever," Jason replied.

Jason grabbed her around the waist and pulled her to him. He planted a light kiss on her juicy lips. His hands wandered farther south onto her lush hips. Tiffenie, a bit out of it with the light wine, forgot herself and relaxed her frame onto his narrow body.

The harmless kiss turned into a brightly lit torch. Jason grabbed a succulent globe in each hand and ground his erection into her. Her pajama top was held together by a zipper running from the nape of her neck to midway of her buttocks. Jason pulled the zipper its full length. It fell from around her shoulders exposing cone shaped breasts. He cupped her ripe breasts in both hands and gently sucked on a nipple.

Tiffenie gasped, shock waves cascading from her breast throughout her body. She grinded into him, pulling his mouth from her breast and sucked on his tongue. Tiffenie slide her hands under Jason's shirt and caressed his chest, back and stomach. Jason walked her backward still clutching her hips. They fell onto the love seat, legs intertwined, and that's how they woke to the morning.

Tiffenie rose first. She watched Jason sleep. He seemed relaxed; all the other times he seemed so tensed. "Shoot, I know this man is going to take me to the office party." She smiled to herself.

"**W**hat time is it?" Thelma asked the woman seated in the cab next to her.

A chocolate, busty woman raised her wrist to her glasses and peered at her watch. "It's about four ten. What, like you got something to do, Thelma?"

"Naw. I just wanted to know what time it is, that's all. You got problems with me asking the time, or is you some type of official time keeper?"

"We ain't even goin' to go there, girl. So just chill," Morrine responded.

"I hope this ain't one of those dragon dives with young, ignorant hoodlums running around in Jheri curls talking 'bout they players," Thelma said.

"Oh no, you'll like this place, it's got class," Morrine exclaimed, rolling her eyes the way she did when she thought something was grand. Rummaging through her purse, Morrine produced a joint which she lit and handed to Thelma. At this time in the morning, traffic was nonexistent. The ancient cab lumbered onto the freeway that overlooked the twinkling city.

"Have you made up your mind what you're going to do?" Morrine asked.

Thelma had drifted off to another time and another place. The reefer was good. She came back to reality with a start, "Thanks for blowing my high. I'd almost forgot about all the shit that I'm in." She paused, took another drag from the joint, and said, "How the hell do I know what I'm going to do." She caught herself, "I'm sorry, Morrine, I didn't mean to take it out on you. Morrine, you've been very kind." Wistfully staring at the city below, she said, "I'm not sure just yet, but if I do get out of this shit, a waterfall of gold won't tempt me again."

"I'm not trying to frighten you, Thelma, but them niggas are for real." Morrine shifted in her seat. "We'll discuss this at another time. For now let's relax," she patted Thelma on the thigh.

Thelma tensed. Morrine's hand was rather high up. It made her uncomfortable. The cabby turned and asked Morrine, "Did you say the twelve hundred block of Fairfax Drive?"

"Yeah, it's just off the next exit. Turn right and let us off at the alley," Morrine replied.

There was a wrought iron railing in the alley that led to a bright red door. In response to Morrine's sharp, coded knock, a fierce looking man with a beard answered the door. "Well, hello ladies, go right up," he said in the softest voice. Thelma almost laughed. His voice did not match his appearance. A heavy set woman let them through a door at the top of the stairs that led into the dining area. The room was lined with booths on both sides. Down the center was a gold-colored bar that curved on either end. The wail of soft, tantalizing saxophone floated overhead.

"This is nice," Thelma exclaimed.

A waitress materialized out of the shadows to take their orders. The soothing atmosphere and amorous night began making its claim on her sore body.

"Morrine, how did you find out about this place? I've never heard of it," Thelma asked.

"It's called 'The Hustlers Delight', very exclusive and very cliche. Some old hustlers own it. Private membership only and you have to be screened. My brother turned me on to it."

"Your brother? I didn't know you had a brother," Thelma stated, surprised. She realized that she saw everyone being alone like her. "Where is he?"

"Oh, he's around. I thought that we would run into him by now," Morrine replied. A door opened in the rear and a troop of men filed in. Their dress was commonplace, however their manner was clipped and businesslike.

"Hey big sister, what's the word?" a man asked Morrine. He came directly to the table and pinched Morrine on her round cheeks. She knocked his hand away in mock anger, but held on to his sleeve. Thelma could tell that she was pleased. The man's face next to Morrine's was almost identical except for her darker complexion. Bobby had freckles.

"This is your brother?" Thelma asked. She thought his open smile was intriguing.

"Bobby, this is a friend of mine. Thelma, meet Bobby, Bobby, Thelma."

"Glad to meet you, Thelma," he replied, his tone serious. "Got to go. You need anything Morrine?"

"Naw, I got my own money," Morrine shot back, a little too sharply, thought Thelma. He tugged her short hair, kissed her on the forehead, then disappeared into the shadows.

"He seems nice — he don't seem like the street type," Thelma stated.

"He used to be, but now he's in this Black organization. Bobby's good people. I just don't let him tell me what to do. You see, by me being the oldest and a girl, our parents were really strict on me. I couldn't go anywhere without our parents going through the ceiling. Our parents were killed in an automobile accident. That forced me out of a sheltered world. Can you trip on it? South Side Chicago." She paused, "Well, I began hustling. Bobby feels guilty

even now, and tries to tell me what to do. Shit, it's too late
for all that. At least I'm not on the streets anymore,"
Morrine stated simply. She took a bite of food. It had
arrived steaming hot and looking quite delicious. She
continued, "At one time he was on drugs and stayed in
trouble with the law. He did a two year stint in the joint.
While he was locked down, he got into this secret Black
militant thang. Personally, I think they still hustling, but
it's so slick don't nobody know what they're doing."

A man in a silk floor-length coat, the likes of which
Thelma had never seen, interrupted, saying, "Excuse me,
Morrine, but have you seen Bobby?"

"He just left," Morrine replied.

Thelma noticed a man that resembled Tiffenie's friend
standing and talking to a man at the top of the staircase.
She couldn't be sure — he was in a shadow. He disappeared down the stairs before she could get a closer look.

"Tell him that Tony's looking for him."

"Yeah, yeah. I'll tell 'em," Morrine replied, yawning. The
man turned away and disappeared into the shadows.
Thelma tried to stifle a yawn. It came out with a ven-
geance.

"That yawn was contagious. I've got to go," Thelma
stated.

"Yeah, me too. Think about what we talked about.
Striker ain't as bad as people say. You dealing with Low
Down. He didn't get that name being nice." Morrine
paused to look at Thelma under veiled eyelids. "I'll see
you Thursday."

Back in her apartment, Thelma lay flat on her back,
looking up into pitch-black darkness. She sensually
cupped her breasts and tweaked both nipples, a ripple of
warmth caused her hips to squirm. How long has it been?

She tried to count the months. They blended into almost a
year. Wonder if Jomo's nice. She still was not sure if she
wanted Jomo to call her. Yeah, I want him to call. She
thought about the way Morrine's brother tugged her hair
and planted a brotherly kiss on her forehead. That was
nice. I'm even jealous of that. An old pimp had once told
her that a woman needed more affection then a child. He's
right, but there was so much fear involved in affection, at
least for her.

   Thelma reflected back on the days when she used to sit
securely on her grandmother's porch in the summertime.
She could feel the sway of the porch swing that everyone
had in that part of Kansas. Her world was her grandmother. It was good things to eat and her two best
friends. George Washington Jones. That name. The
thought of him brought a smile to her lips. George was
her brother. She remembered making mud pies with
Willie Mae, wrestling with George, and getting spankings
'cause little girls don't play roughhouse with little boys.
Not in Grandma's house. The summer heat simmered off
those country roads like heat rising from a oven. She
remembered her grandmother's friends, and how they
kept vigil over her casket. The old men had set her casket
before the large picture window in the front room. The
perfume that Sister Clarice wore brought back those
memories. All of her grandmother's friends were very old.
After her grandmother passed, there wasn't anyone left to
take care of her. When she turned eighteen, she left Kansas City State Orphanage to visit her old home town.
George was long gone. She was told that he had killed a
state trooper somewhere in Tennessee. George mysteri-
ously died or had been killed in jail. The town had become
just a memory for most of the young people who had
moved on. The elders had all but died out. The town

grocery store had long since been abandoned due to lack of cliental. The store was boarded up. Some teens passing through for the summer, had destroyed many of the old landmarks, including the old store. The only usable remnant was the porch swing of her grandmother's house. It was suspended from the ceiling by rusted chains. The paint was pealing from the once white-washed wooden swing. It was swaying in the light August wind as if it was mocking her.

With that thought, she reached under her pillow and retrieved her vibrator. The faint buzzing against her pubic mound caused her hips to squirm. Moaning aloud, she reached a climax, trying to imagine what it would be like to be with Jomo. It was Bobby's face that replaced his. Vaguely, it seemed that she saw Jason's form in a shadow before drifting off to sleep.

The shrill ring of her phone brought her into a murky light. With her shades drawn, the sunniest day could be blotted out. "Hello," she answered, still drowsy.

"Yo girlfriend, what you doin' in bed?" Tiffenie's cheery tone caused her to sit up on one elbow.

"Where are you?" she asked.

"I'm at work. It's two o'clock in the afternoon. You're off tonight, aren't you?"

"Yeah, but it's still too early for me to think right. I'll call you back."

"That's all right, I'll be over after work. Don't get cute with me, girl, I haven't seen you in ages."

Tiffenie's cheeriness caused her to laugh outright.

"OK, I'll be here. Bring some wine with you. You know that I don't let bums in my house," Thelma answered, reeling from Tiffenie's raucous laughter that hurt her ears.

After her night people's lunch, as she called it, around three fifteen, the phone rang again. Thelma, standing with her arms crossed in her kitchen, unfolded them and walked deliberately to the phone. "Yes, this is the Watkins residence," she answered.

"Well hello, Mrs. Queen of Egypt, how 'bout a little ride down The Nile?" the voice answered back, mimicking her formal tone.

"Jomo!" she shouted, recognizing his voice. Relief flooded her, "Well, you finally called." Thelma caught herself. She definitely didn't want Jomo to get the wrong impression.

"Hey, is everything all right? Has that guy from the party bothered you?"

"No, he hasn't bothered me. I appreciate your concern." There was a pause. "When you goin' to take me somewhere, nigga? And I don't mean to Burger King."

Jomo's soft deep laughter could be heard over the receiver, "Let's do something this weekend during the day. You ever play put-put?" he asked.

"Yes, I've played put-put before. It's fun. How about if Jason and Tiffenie come along?"

"That sounds good. I'll call you tomorrow and establish a time. Got to run. See you, Thelma."

Thelma found herself smiling broadly. Yes. She had a date with a man. The world was not all gloom and doom. She wondered if it was premature to invite Jason and Tiff. Maybe she should have cleared it with Tiff first. She liked Jomo but she did not want to be alone with him as yet.

A sudden knock at her door caused her heart to quicken to a bird's pace. The way her buzzer was placed, you had to buzz her apartment in order to get into the building. Who was at her door?

Hairbrush in hand, she rushed into her bedroom and quickly changed into baggy jeans and sweat shirt. Undecided, she finally pulled a Berreta 380 from beneath her mattress and placed it in her waist band. On tiptoes, she crept to the hall door and bent to look under the door. A pair of upside down eyes met her stare.

"Open the door, Thelma. It's Boone and Striker," Boone's voice rang out.

What can happen? They need me to work, she reasoned. With more confidence then she imagined she had, she swung open the door and ushered them in saying, "Come right on in and have a seat. And, by the way, I really don't appreciate anyone coming to my house uninvited."

Striker Newvel was dressed in a grey silk suit with matching grey silk shirt, grey socks, and grey leather shoes. It was said that he had enough grey suits to open his own clothing store. Clean shaven, a smooth chocolate color, Striker was a class act, cold, ruthless, and suave with a dazzling smile. The odd thing about his smile was that most people did not smile back, it might have been his vibes. His smile was strong and deeply distorted. Stiker enjoyed brutality; he enjoyed invoking fear. That was his shortcoming. He simply got too much enjoyment out of the distasteful chores of his trade. Nevertheless, Striker controlled the go between the law makers and law breakers. It was a big, corrupt city with millions of dollars of illegal money floating around. Stiker saw to it that it floated in his direction.

"We're so sorry, Thelma, and it won't ever happen again." He flashed that wide open sunny/sinister smile, then continued. "We just got some information that the people across town want to offer you a big contract. I just want to protect my interest and want us to maintain a productive and mutually satisfying working arrangement. May we sit at the table? I'd like for you to take a look at something that our lawyer has drawn up for you."

"Sure, have a seat on the couch. I'll pull up a chair."

"Oh no, you might hurt yourself. Boone will get the chair for you. Won't you, Boone," he said pointedly.

"Sure, sure, Mr. Newvel. No problem," Boone said, scurrying to push the chair up to the coffee table.

Thelma would have thought Boone flopping around was funny except for this Striker guy. She sensed he wasn't anything nice, but he was a business man. Her brain began to whirl. "When was this drawn up, Mr. Dewvel?"

"To be perfectly honest with you, Thelma, the contract was drawn up about a month ago. I've had my lawyer spice it up and I'm presenting it to you now. Like I said before, to protect my interest." He paused. "Thelma, please call me Striker, all my friends do. And Thelma, we are going to be good friends."

Striker slid a brown folder across the table. He watched Thelma closely, trying to detect which way she would go. Her eyebrow arched. Got her now, he thought.

Freakin' me, Thelma thought. Hope he don't notice my pulse racing. They going to pay me that kind of money for dancing. Her heart turned cold. Don't get something for nothing. There had to be a catch to this.

"Striker, if I understand this contract correctly, you're going to pay me almost three thousand dollars a week. I'll have you paid off, what is the real deal?"

"The deal is, Thelma, you're hot. You're a sensation. We've never raked in this kind of money at our club before until you started dancing for us. We're just sharing the wealth, hoping that you would become a willing partner. And, if you noticed in the contract, you don't owe me anything — that's all taken care of. There are no gimmicks, no games. The contract says for four more weeks. Then if you like, and I'm really serious," he paused, "if you like, we'll draw up a contract and sponsor you not only all over this country, but in international tours as well."

Thelma quickly calculated that she could walk out of this place with at least six grand in her pocket. I'll disappear on these monkeys, she thought.

"I'll sign, Striker, but in four weeks, if I want to skate, you got to let me"?

"You have my word, Thelma, but we're going to try to make it hard for you to turn our next offer down."

As soon as Thelma signed the document, Stiker smoothly put it in his brief case and motioned Boone to the door. "Next time, I'll be sure to call first," he said while tipping his hat.

After the door closed, Thelma breathed a sigh of relief. She reexamined her copy of the contract again. Nothing, no clause, nothing. According to this document, she was free after four weeks of work. She knew that there was more to it than was meeting the eye, but shit, she would disappear on these monkeys. "Won't even leave moon dust," she said aloud. The hands on the clock read four-thirty. Tiff should be here in the next hour. They would celebrate.

"I don't get it. If you care about the man and he cares about you..." Thelma paused before she could finish her sentence. Tiffenie cut in.

"What am I supposed to do, live off his security guard salary? I went to school and I have a right to use it," Tiffenie explained, waving her hands, her voice rising.

Thelma leaned back blowing smoke at the ceiling. "I ain't Jason, so you don't have to get uptight with me, girlfriend." A smile crept onto her lips. Tiffenie laughed, seeming relieved.

Thelma served Tiffenie a tall glass of ice tea, complete with a slice of lemon. Tiff seemed uptight about something. Thelma would just have to wait until her friend told her what the real deal was. Meanwhile, they were just chillin', playing music.

"By the way, where is the wine, girlfriend?"

"Oh, I forgot to get it downtown, and those guys standing around the liquor store in this neighborhood made me nervous."

"Did they say anything to you?" Thelma asked, wrinkles appearing on her forehead.

"Just the usual, 'hey mamma, what's your phone number' and all that street stuff," she answered.

"So what upset you?"

Tiffenie paused, "Well," she began slowly, "it seems like they hate me or resent me and one of those guys reminds me so much of my brother. I looked up to say hi and his eyes seemed to be on fire. They frightened me by being so hopeless, just milling around in front of that store all day.

Some of them stand around the bus station in the morning where I go to work. It frightens me, Thelma. I really don't know why but it does."

Thelma leaned forward in her chair, "This is the first time that you've mentioned your brother, girlfriend." Thelma stood and walked across the room to where Tiffenie was sitting. "You are going to have to get a grip. Maybe your world is the one that's frightening, because you're beginning to realize how narrow it is and, more importantly, how little control you have over it. Just might be that we're all milling around in front of somebody's store just waiting for something to happen."

Tiffenie did not answer. She sat deep in thought. "My brother was everything to me," she began. "I can remember when I was a little girl, Stanley would take me to the store with him. It was like I was on top of the world. He could run faster than everybody in the neighborhood except for Lionel Peabody. I hated Lionel. You know how it is when you have a brother."

"Yeah, I know how it is," Thelma replied. She recalled her relationship with George Washington.

"Well, after his first year at college, he began to change. He become angry. My father and Stanley had a terrible argument. Stanley left home and he just seemed to fade away. The next thing we knew, he was on drugs in Philadelphia. That hurt me. It still does. Every time I see a bunch of Brothers standing around on a corner, I think of my brother."

"I want some alcohol." Thelma said, breaking the mood. "We can walk to the state store and get some. Just give me a sec to slip something on and I'll be right with you."

While Thelma was changing, Tiffenie turned and caught her reflection in the mirror that covered an entire wall of the apartment. There were wrinkles that she had not noticed. She realized that she had been living under a lot of pressure. Not just the length of time that she had moved to the big city, but ever since she had left Michael for something 'better'. She was sure that her feelings for Michael had passed, but the thought of that type of sacrifice for someone that you really cared about just because of peer pressure, was just too much. He wasn't in school, he didn't play sports, all the trash that her girl friends had talked about him.... Her thoughts were cut short as Thelma exited her bedroom. "Let's go get some fuel, girl, before you burn out."

The cool breeze on Tiffenie's forehead calmed her considerably. She slowed her pace to match her shorter companion's gait. The aroma of collard greens and corn bread wafted out of an upstairs window. Someone was playing Stevie Wonder's *Living for the City.'* Her stomach began to turn flip flops. Tiffenie had not eaten since lunch. As the two women turned onto the next street, Tiffenie realized that they would have to pass the men lounging around on the corner. Thelma watched Tiffenie from the corner of her eye. She began walking forcefully, her heels beating out a distinct rhythm on the sidewalk.

"Hold up a minute, Tiff."

To Tiffenie's surprise, the man who reminded her of her brother greeted Thelma with a friendly, "How the finest woman of East Street?"

"I'm good. How you doin', jitterbug?" Thelma replied.

"Girl, you know I'm just out here free-lancing," he stated, cocking his head to one side and profiling.

Tiffenie, who had been standing back, moved forward. The long black coat with tennis shoes sort of looked good in a street kind of way. He was kind of handsome, Tiffenie thought.

Thelma turned and introduced the two. Tiffenie smiled and nodded her head. The name Jamal fit him. Meanwhile, some of the other men began clustering around the trio. Thelma continued her introductions. "This is Pee Wee, Akium, and Leroy.

The man called Akium stepped forward and said, "What's up, sister love? I've seen you around the hood once or twice. I'm honored to meet you." He turned to Thelma and said, "I got some of that lighthouse smoke. You up for it?"

"All I got is a twenty. Can you break it in half for me?"

"S-h-o-o-w. Just step around to my office."

Ducking into a nearby doorway, the two made a quick exchange. Thelma, beckoning to Tiffenie, waved airily to the troop of men as they made their way up the street. On their way back from the liquor store, Thelma and Tiffenie were so absorbed in their conversation, neither noticed the beat-up, yellow Cadillac rolling smoothly behind them. A man with deep scratches on his face drove the car.

It was twilight and the sun's rays were only a faint light against the city's skyline. Bursting into Thelma's apartment, Tiffenie rushed to the bathroom. When she returned, a liter of Coke and a bottle of Hennessey were neatly arranged on the coffee table.

Thelma, coming from the kitchen with a tray of ice said, "At least those thugs at the corner didn't mug us." Her voice was filled with ridicule.

Tiffenie, sipping her amber drink, just shook her head. She began, "I realize that I have a lot of catching up to do. College, in a way deceived me. I used to think that all I had to do was study real hard, keep my figure, maintain a

smooth complexion, and the world would be mine." She
paused. "Well tell me, Mrs. Know-it-All, what's real?"

"All I know is, when it's winter, you got to have heat and
when you're hungry, you got to eat — everything in between are luxuries," Thelma answered, the corners of her
mouth turning down.

"Oh, come off of it, Thelma. You know there's got to be
more than that. If that's all there was to life, we'd be no
more than animals." Tiffenie paused to sip her drink. "I
got needs that I didn't know I had. Remember the first
night that we went out?

"How could I forget. We got gangster hits out on us for
jumping on one of the biggest dope boys in the city,"
Thelma stated smiling.

"That shit ain't funny. I'm not talking about the party.
I'm talking about our conversation at the night club." It
was Tiffenie's turn to stand, fold her arms and pace back
and forth in front of Thelma. "I might not know a lot
about those streets out there, but there are some things I
do know. I can tell when someone is jiving me, sisterlove,
and you, my sister, is jiving me. I'm not ashamed to say it.
I need people. I need you as a friend. I need Jason as a
friend, lover and a man."

At intervals, she would stop in front of Thelma and
gesture with her arms and hands, and then stand silently
trying to catch Thelma's gaze. "The only difference between you and me is that I'm not afraid to say I need.
This friendship has to go two ways," she said, folding her
arms to punctuate the statement.

Thelma avoided Tiffenie's penetrating stare by looking
into her drink. She began slowly mouthing her words
carefully, "I've been afraid to ask or expect anything. The
only peace that I've had was with my grandmother in the
sticks of Kansas. I never knew my mother. She abandoned

me and my grandmother when I was two years old. After my grandmother died, I ended up in an orphanage for five years. All I ever wanted was a family, a house, my own bed and to know for sure that somebody cared. I ain't got none of that and, yes Tiff, I'll admit it —.I am afraid. You know, I didn't sleep with a man until I was twenty-three." Thelma rose suddenly to face her guest knocking over her drink, the liquid spilling onto her maroon carpet. She continued, "Did you know that contract I showed you is a con? Ain't no way Striker Newvel is going to let me out of this town. We ain't even talking 'bout good-hearted Low Down. I was going to just skip town and be a ghost to you and everybody else. And, hell yes Tiff, I need somebody and I want somebody to care about me. Who gives a fuck if somebody fishes me out of a river?"

"I care, but you have to take the chance that somebody will go all the way with you. You've got to know that it's what you deserve. When I jumped into that fight, it was not only for you, it was for me too. Thelma, you got to take the chance that I'll love you forever, but you got to give it up." Abrupt silence followed her speech. The only sounds were from the traffic in the street below.

"First, I want to know everything about this Striker deal, and Thelma, I want all of it," Tiffenie demanded.

Thelma's secretive life was laid bare. She explained the tug of war between the uptown guys and Striker and her role in it. When Tiffenie realized that Thelma had initially planned to just disappear, she almost lost it.

"You slurp. You actually mean that you were going to leave and not tell me? I knew you were planning some stuck-on-stupid stuff. It's a good thing that I got my African-motherhood, intuition-groove flowing. Something told me to come by here and check on you."

"You killin' me now, Tiff." Thelma stood in mock protest.
"And what's a slurp?"

"I'd of killed you if you'd left without telling me."

"I think that you're overreacting now, girlfriend,"
Thelma stated, seeming relieved.

"Well, I'm going to tell Jason about it," Tiffenie. "Maybe
he can work out some type of deal for us."

"Yeah, the police will fish all three of us out of Span
Dike Lake," Thelma replied.

"Don't say stuff like that. It's bad luck," Tiffenie admonished. A gloom settling over the room. Quiet again filled
the apartment, both women absorbed in thought.

Tiffenie glanced at her watch, "Got to go. I didn't realize
that it was so late. Jason was supposed to come by or call.
I'll see you this weekend. Remember, we're supposed to
play put-put as couples. I like miniature golf. Jason will
too. You'll see, we'll have a grand time."

Thelma grasped Tiffenie to her and bear-hugged her at
the door. "Yeah. We beat that mutha's ass," Tiffenie
stated in the hall, shadow boxing in front of the elevator.
Thelma closed the door laughing.

The only occupants on the street were eerie, long shadows losing their form into blackened alleyways. Except for
the occasional whisk of cars, the only sound was the
tapping of her heels on the pavement. Tiffenie wondered
how Jason would fare at the company dinner. A car door
opening just behind her did not call for undue alarm, but
the last footstep just behind her did. An oily hand clapped
over her mouth as an unyielding arm snatched her backward.

Her senses reeled as she desperately flung her body from
side to side trying to break the hold. Tiffenie saw another
arm open the car door. Comprehending what their inten-

tions were, she bit deeply into the palm that was cutting off her breath. A howl of pain lifted the quiet off the empty streets. Out of the corner of her eye, as if in slow motion, she watched a gloved fist explode in a bright orange light across her eyelids. Suddenly, the arms that held her released their hold. She dimly saw a long dark coat and sneakers as the pavement came rushing up to meet her. Instinct instructed her to break her fall, but her limbs would not obey. A hoarse shout, then gunshots rang out. Tiffenie surrendered to the weight pressing down between her ears.

She regained a portion of her senses among flashing red lights and white-garbed ambulance attendants. The street was thronged with curious bystanders, many of the women had curlers in their hair. Slowly, Jason's features came into focus. He was bending over her. Surprisingly his expression was calm.

"Tiffenie. Tiffenie, can you hear me? Don't try to answer. I'm with you now and you're safe."

She tried to respond, but speech just would not come to her lips. He stroked her forehead gently. Tiffenie was aware of being lifted into the interior of the ambulance, then a soft welcome darkness.

Jason stood with his hands hanging at his sides, talking with the attending physician. The brightly lit hospital corridor hurt his eyes, causing him to squint. "Yes, the concussion seems minor. However, we'll know more in the morning," the white-coated doctor replied.

"What about her jaw?" Jason asked.

"It's not broken. She'll just be a little sore for a couple of days. In cases like this, it's not the physical damage that I'd worry about. It's the trauma of the incident. Tiffenie

will just have to take one day at a time," the doctor answered. He turned and briskly walked down the hall.

A cold knot had worked its way into the pit of Jason's
stomach. He had not felt this way since he had seen his
comrades blown to bits by their own artillery in the Gulf.
This was much more. He realized that for most of his life,
he had been a loner. Now, with Tiffenie, things were
different; he could be hurt and crippled by being close to
another person. Helpless, that's how he felt. Helpless. If
that man, Jamal, had not intervened... He was afraid to
speculate the consequences. There was one fact that he
knew — Tiffenie would not have to worry about Low
Down anymore.

A man with pinpoint eyes walked directly toward him.
Those eyes were embedded in folds of flesh. There was a
bulge below his left arm pit. A neon sign with 'COP' flashing on his forehead would not have been more effective
than that rain coat he was wearing. Jason turned and
faced him, placing his right foot slightly to the rear.

"You a Mister Jason Carter?" he asked.

"Yes, that's me. May I help you, Detective?" Jason replied. The detective's eyebrows shot upward.

"Mr. Carter, I'm Detective Shultz, and I've been assigned
to this case." He paused to pull a notebook from his rear
pants pocket and a pen from the inside of his rain coat.
"What exactly is your relationship to Mrs. Young?"

"She's my woman," Jason replied, watching Shultz carefully.

"Were you at the scene at the time of the assault?"

"No, I came after I heard gunfire. I was looking for
Tiffenie. When she didn't show up at her place, I figured
she'd be at Thelma's."

"Did you know the man who was killed, a Jamal Nooks?"

"No, when did he die? I thought that he was just wounded."

"He died just a few minutes ago. A large caliber gunshot to the chest is usually fatal," Shultz added. His features narrowed suspiciously, seeing the bulge under Jason's left armpit. "Is your firearm registered?"

"Of course, that's my line of work. I'm a security guard for Florsheim Security Service," Jason explained. A faint smile tugged at the corners of Shultz's lips.

"I'd like you to come down to the police station and go through some mug shots. That is, if you're up to it." Shultz asked.

"I'll be down in the morning. If the mug shots don't add up, maybe we can come up with a composite."

"Very well, Mr. Carter. I see that you're familiar with police procedures. Ever been in any trouble with the law?"

"No, never," Jason curtly replied.

"I'll be looking forward to seeing you in the morning, about eight-thirty."

Jason turned and headed toward the waiting room. He felt Shultz's eyes on him.

The waiting room was filled with an array of Friday night accidents. Housewives surrounded by impatient children, teenagers puffing on cigarettes. Trying hard to be cool. Some of the emergency room patients had contrived makeshift bandages which were soaked with blood; the result of their latest adventures.

Carefully scanning the assorted crowd in the hospital, Jason instantly spied Jomo's Rhasta braids. He was standing over Thelma and whispering into her ear. What ever he was telling her, each sentence was being emphasized by the recoil of his tightly braided hair.

Thelma spotted Jason and rose quickly. "How is Tiff, and don't even try to lie."

"Tiffenie's fine. In fact, the doctor feels that, if she can deal with the emotional shock, she'll be one hundred percent in a couple of days," Jason replied, trying to sound as confident as the doctor.

"We got to throw down, Jason," Jomo interrupted, a gravel edge to his voice.

"We'll talk about that when we get out of here, Jomo," Jason replied quickly. He noted that Jomo's eyes were gleaming the way they used to before a fight in high school.

Jason continued, "We can't do anything for her now. She's so deeply sedated, she won't know anything until late tomorrow. Let's go to my place. We need to talk."

Jason's apartment was near the river on the south side of town. The apartment consisted of a single room with a fold out sofa bed; an alcove, housing a stove and refrigerator; and a surprisingly large bathroom. Thelma and Jomo sat on the bed facing Jason, who had pulled up the single folding chair.

"Let's get our heads going in one direction," Jason began, then paused. "This Low Down guy is a sick individual and he has to be dealt with discreetly and decisively."

"It really don't have to be a big conference to decide what to do, Jason," Jomo abruptly cut in. "We got to put this guy in the hall of fame. Look Jason, this guy knows that we know what he tried to do. His mentality is thinking that we're out to get him no matter what. If we don't get him, he will get us." He imitated Jason's mother standing and waving his hands. "Or Jason, do you think we can invite him over for a cup of tea and iron out our differences?"

Jason, his eyes never leaving Jomo's, said, "It's *my* woman. How do you *think* I feel? I wish that we had more alternatives, but after tonight, I have to agree with you, Jomo. Low Down will be taken care of and it's important that..." He paused to get their undivided attention. "...this conversation never took place." Jason took a deep breath, then continued, "Jomo, I want you to be highly visible. This cop, Shultz, he has me worried." The sentence lingered in mid air.

Thelma had been sitting quietly. "Wait a minute, Jason. My main concern at this time is Tiffenie. Do you think that she is safe in the hospital? How about waiting until she gets well, then getting our asses out of town. What y'all talking 'bout sounds good, but Low Down has an organization and backup. All we have is us. It's not a good match. I say let's just disappear." She stated this very softly, mouthing each word carefully. Thelma's antenna was up, She felt that Jason was not telling them everything. She watched him closely. "Exactly what did happen, Jason?" Only her eyes revealed her suspicions.

"This is what happened." Jason began. "I was supposed to call Tiffenie, but I got tied up and was much longer than I had anticipated. I rode over to her place. She wasn't home. I waited around some, then I walked over to Thelma's hoping to catch her there. When I turned the corner, I saw a man in a long black coat and tennis shoes wrestling with a man alongside of a yellow Caddy. When I got closer, I saw Tiffenie laying in the street. A man got out of the rear of the Caddy and shot dude. He acted like he was going to pick up Tiffenie. Then I drew my revolver and began shooting into the air. He got back in the car and they sped off. A woman across the street saw everything and she had already called the police before I got there. They arrived just after the yellow Caddy pulled off. Dude is dead. His name was Jamal Nooks."

"Jamal!" Thelma screamed. She hid her face in her hands and began to cry.

"Did you know this man?" Jason asked, a bit surprised.

"Yeah, he hung out in the hood. I introduced him to Tiff on the way to the liquor store today. Jamal was always a good person. Why do bad things have to happen because of me?" Thelma asked, tears glistening on her cheeks. Jomo wrapped his arms around her. He said, "You can't blame yourself. Shit happens," he added.

She quit sobbing and looked at Jason. "Why are you worried about the police, Jason? You ain't into nothing are you?"

"It's not that, Thelma. This cop will come down hard on me if anything happens to Low Down, and I don't have a good alibi. I just want things to work out for the best, that's all. Look, Jomo is going to stay around your place as long as you need him. There are a lot of things that I have to do," Jason stated.

Silence prevailed in the tiny apartment. Jason walked Thelma and Jomo downstairs and watched them disappear around the corner.

Jason donned his jacket and began walking. He had called Bobby earlier and made a ten o'clock appointment. It was still early and he had a lot of time to kill. He caught the bus downtown. He had promised to pick up some medicine for his mother. Once in the drug store, he had to search for the type of cream that his mother used for her skin. Finally, after canvassing the store the second time around, he found it — 'Cream of New Orleans.' He had never seen nor heard of the product anywhere but his mother's house. There was a tingling sensation that tickled his ears; someone was following him. Looking out of the corner of his eye, he noticed a man attired in a light brown rain coat, watching him.

Jason smiled at the man, then walked to the counter to purchase the cream. Just as he stepped out of the store, one plainclothesman and two uniformed security guards stopped him.

"Look Buddy, we don't want no trouble. Just open your coat. We have to search you."

Jason complied.

"Well, it looks like you're clean. Sorry for the inconvenience," the plainclothes cop said.

"Hey Officer, I don't feel bad when white men accuse me of stealing. After all, that's how *you* got everything that you got." Jason paused to test their reaction. They looked shocked. "After all, you stole *me*, remember?" Jason continued walking down the street laughing at their stares of disbelief.

Jason remembered the first time that he had been followed and stopped by security police. He had been
stopped, searched, and told that, if he did not want to buy
anything, to stay on his side of town. There was a job
interview that he was supposed to go to that day. Jason
was dumbfounded. Instead of going to the interview, he
caught the bus home. Once in his bedroom, his entire
body shook. It felt as if someone had spit on him. What
was really degrading was the casual attitude of the police.

He'd been naive then, uneducated to his relationship to
the means and mode of production. No longer was he
shocked or angry. They, as a people, were in a constant
state of war. It was a fact of life that he had finally accepted. Jason had stayed in his room the next couple of
days. Once he got the resolve to start looking for a job
again, he promised himself that he would never accept
the position that this society had regulated for him.

He laughed out loud as he reflected on the times that he
and Jomo enjoyed in high school. The fights, the women
they had chased, the cheap wine and the laughter. That's
what Tiffenie had brought to his world, laughter. The idea
of Tiffenie in a hospital bed caused him to stop. A cold
knot gripped his stomach, and the anger that he was
trying to control surfaced full force. This ball could not be
fumbled. She had come into his life from out of nowhere.
Now a man had tried to hurt or kill her. The thought was
reprehensible. Low Down had better have made plans
'cause he was sure going to meet his maker.

Jason had been discharged from the service for seven
months before he found out about the 'Organization.'
While playing pool at a neighborhood hall, he noticed a
poster on the wall. It depicted a Black man and woman
standing back to back with rifles in their hands. Large
letters had read, 'We stand ready to die for the dignity of

a people.' At the bottom of the poster had been an address and time for a rally. At the rally, there were about thirty to forty people present. Their political platform was simple — to organize the people into an organ to seize power *'By Any Means Necessary.'* The literacy program was sound. It allowed the Black men and women in the community who wanted to make a positive contribution to do so. Jason had thrown himself into the political education classes wholeheartedly. The classes were held every Thursday night at Mr. Miller's house.

He was so impressed with the speaker and the party rhetoric, that he volunteered to help with the city-wide literacy program. It was there that he meet Bobby. Never would he have known the depth, seriousness, or complexity of The Organization so quickly if not for Bobby. He was introduced to the 'Society of the Copper and Steel,' which was the Organization's version of an army and an intelligence bureau. Neither Tiffenie nor Jomo knew anything about The Organization. Eventually, he would have to tell Tiffenie something. Most people thought The Organization was single faceted; that they just developed and implemented social programs, like the literacy program. The organization was much more. He felt alive just to be a part of it.

The problem was how to eliminate Low Down without causing undue attention to himself. He glanced at his watch— he had another hour. Jason decided to take the medicine over to his mother's house, then attend his rendezvous. This problem of Low Down would be resolved one way or another.

Across town, looking out of his office window, Detective Shultz stood with his hands clasped behind his back. His office window overlooked the alley that stood beside one of

the largest hotels in the city. His view was of large, green
dumpsters.

"Inspector Shultz, the information on Jason Carter is
in," a voice crackled over his intercom.

Turning from the window, Shultz pushed the rubber
knob with his index finger and replied, "Tell someone to
bring it up and get Lieutenant Flippo in here."

A young Cadet just in from the police academy brought
in a manila folder. Unlike Shultz, he was neat and professional looking. Flippo, his chief assistant and friend, came
in eating a foul smelling fish sandwich and sporting a
blue suit with a purple shirt and bright blue tie. The suit
and tie combination, in most circles, would be considered
bad taste. Shultz thought it looked good.

"What are you're eating? Smells like shit, Flippo."

"This is a good sandwich, Inspector. You should try one.
It's fresh mushrooms, and soho beans. All that red meat
and sugar you eat will kill you. You'll be dead at sixty
from your diet," Flippo answered between mouthfuls.

"Well, I'll die in peace, Flippo."

"Did you get a chance to read the dossier on this Carter
fellow?" Shultz asked, his tone serious.

"Yeah, I read it. Nothing. This guy got an honorable
discharge from the Marine Corps, does not have a political
history that we know of, and does not have a criminal
history of any kind whatsoever. We even checked his high
school record. Nothing, not a grain of salt or speck of
pepper. If I may say so, Inspector, the time and manpower
we spent investigating this guy was a waste. Next time
bells go off in your head take an aspirin and call me in the
morning."

"I can't help it, Flippo. Something's up with this guy.
Well, let's go over that crime scene again. It was a profes-

sional job. By the way, what did this Jason Carter do in the Marine Corps?"

Flippo folded what was left of his sandwich in waxed paper and picked up the folder. He thumbed through it slowly. "Inspector. Guess what?

"What, Flippo," Shultz answered, exasperation in his voice.

"He was a small arms and explosive specialist." The two men's eyes met.

"How much money was taken in that armored car robbery?" Shultz asked.

"About five hundred thousand dollars," Flippo responded. Flippo began unwrapping his sandwich, took a bite, then continued, "The guy has a run down car, lives in a flea-bit apartment and works for $7.57 an hour. Look Inspector, if you get something on this guy that's tangible, we'll keep an eye on him. Other than that, let's follow the leads that we do have. They don't lead anywhere in his direction."

Shultz continued looking out of the window at the alley below. Flippo closed the door softly behind him.

The room was slightly chilly, as all hospital rooms go. To keep down viruses and germs, at least that's what the staff tells you. Bottom line, winter or summer, hospitals are cold, much too cold for her liking. These were Tiffenie's thoughts waking up in the middle of the night. She vaguely remembered Jason's face and voice on the street, then being lifted into the ambulance and then darkness. She turned one way then another, gingerly testing her muscles. A sharp twinge ran down her lower back. She relaxed and tried to use those muscles again. It twinged, but not as bad as the first time. She'd be all right. Tiffenie breathed a sigh of relief. Suddenly, it dawned on her. Men, more than one, had tried to kidnap or kill her. "Shoot, I'm a female James Bond," she giggled aloud.

One of the shadows that had lain dormant merged into a human form, Tiffenie inhaled to scream. A hand clamped down on her mouth.

"Shut up, girl. You knew that I would come and see you after work.

"Thelma, you almost scared me to death, and I mean it," Tiffenie groaned.

"I've been worried sick, Tiff. How do you feel?" Thelma whispered.

"I'm OK, Thelma, just a little sore, and my face and neck hurt. Other than that I'm going to be fine."

"When Jason called me to come down to the hospital, I almost passed out. We got to get you well, Tiff. Jason and Jomo talkin' 'bout doin' Dude. What we need to do is to get gone, but you got to get well first."

"I'm getting sick of this shit, Thelma. I don't see why we can't go to the police. Hey, this Low Down is a confirmed criminal. Both of us pay taxes. I'm not wanted for anything, neither are you," Tiffenie stated.

"You'd better hold off, Tiff, 'cause your man Jason is in to something. I don't know what exactly, but the way that he ran it to Jomo and Me, he can't afford no police scrutiny. Better check up on your man, girlfriend." Thelma paused, then hugged Tiffenie to her. "You know that I'm not supposed to be in here," she continued.

"How did you get in?" Tiffenie asked.

"I got a nurse's coat for one of my acts. I just walked in hoping they wouldn't notice my white high heels." Both women giggled uncontrollably.

"Oh, that hurt," said Tiffenie, grimacing.

"That's my cue. Got to go, Tiff. You know I had to find out for myself how you were." With a swift hug, Thelma disappeared back into the shadows and Tiffenie drifted into a deep sleep.

Jason began climbing the stairs exactly three minutes before he was due at the rendezvous. Bobby opened the door before he could knock. Jason was surprised by the sight of eight men sitting around the tiny apartment. He nodded his head, but got no response.

"Hey Jason, let me talk to you in the kitchen," Bobby invited.

Like in his apartment, the kitchen was no more than a cubbie hole. "They already knew, they came to me. This is big shit, Jason, this is the Central Crew," Bobby whispered tensely.

"What does the Central Crew got to do with this?" Jason whispered.

"You'll know everything as soon as we get started," Bobby answered, his voice regaining its normal tone.

Jason helped Bobby rearrange the kitchen chairs into somewhat of a circle in the front room.

Bobby stood as if at attention. "Junior Officer seeks permission to address the main council," he asked.

"Permission granted, Bobby," a squat brown-skinned man answered. His nose looked like it had suffered some mishaps. Jason wondered if he might have been a boxer in his youth. He sat erect, and seemed to be in charge.

"Jason, Junior Officer of the Intelligence Bureau, has run into a dilemma, which concerns his woman and a street gangster named Low Down. It seems that Low Down got into a free-for-all with a woman named Thelma. Tiffenie, Jason's woman, jumped in. The day before yesterday, Low Down, or some of his boys, beat ol' girl down, and tried to kidnap her. Jason wants Low Down hit, but does not want undo attention drawn to himself." Bobby, after giving what sounded like a lawyer's delivery, stood still with his hands clasped behind his back.

Mr. Miller, the man that Jason had identified as being in charge, stood with his hands hanging loosely at his sides. "I'll be quick and to the point. At this time in our operation, it would be untimely to get any type of surveillance directed toward any of our operations or on The Organization as a whole. Now, this Low Down is no small-fry and we do not, in any way, take him lightly. However, he is not the fish we would like to fry. Dewvel is who we really want. We have discussed Jason's situation and realize that his woman friend and Thelma are in danger.

"I'll have to agree with the young man, we are too close to draw any unwarranted attention.

"Thelma won't have anything to worry about for now. Our information sources tell us that Dewvel has promised Thelma to Low Down as soon as he's done with her. As long as she is making Dewvel money, we won't have to worry about her, but we feel that shortly afterward he is going to have her killed. So the immediate danger is with this Tiffenie." He paused and swept his gaze around the room, then continued. "My suggestion is that we deal with Low Down and Striker Dewvel immediately." He stopped talking abruptly and sat down.

The other men at the table nodded their heads in approval. Jason looked to Bobby for clarification. Bobby simply waved his hands. The meeting was finished.

The men began filing out of the room. "Bobby, you and Jason wait here. I'll be right back up. I'm going to walk these gentlemen downstairs," Miller stated.

"What the fuck is going on, Bobby? You're going to have to tell me something. What has The Organization got to do with Dewvel, anyway?"

Before Bobby could answer, Miller slipped back into the room. "Have a seat, both of you, and please just listen," Miller stated, waving them to a seat.

"Jason, I know you're a bit in the dark. Let me enlighten you," he began, once he was seated. "This Organization that you've joined is ready for a quantum leap. That means that it's imperative that we gain access to more capital. You see, wealth, as we define it, is the ability to expand one's culture to its maximum capacity. I'm sure that you'll both agree Black folks are long overdue. The struggle is the same struggle that took place 40,000 years ago — the acquisition of territory in order to exploit its resources in the interest of your species.

"We have to stay incognito, especially now. In a few years, five to be exact, we'll be able to solidify our assets and cash into viable legitimate businesses."

Miller stood, paced around the room, then said, "Jason, I know it's your girlfriend and you're emotionally tied to her, but when you joined this Organization, we stressed that extreme personal sacrifices would have to be made. Fortunately for you, your little escapade came along at an opportune time." He paused and placed his foot on the folding chair, standing over Jason and Bobby. "I want you and Bobby to handle both jobs — on Low Down and a Mr. Dewvel. Make it look like a typical gangster hit and you're out of here. Do I make myself clear, gentlemen?"

Both men nodded their heads.

It had begun to rain lightly. The streets in this part of town were old cobblestone. An automobile, stopping abruptly, could swerve out of control. The years of wear and the rain made the street extremely slick and danger-ous.

Striker Dewvel finished splashing on aftershave. It was Friday and he had decided to relax before going out and checking on his various traps. He donned his robe and, after another glance in his bathroom mirror, yelled out into the front room, "Hey girl, fix me a scotch and tonic."

He didn't wait for a reply and proceeded into his bedroom, which was almost as large as his living room. In the center of the room was a circular bed, and a mirror, as large as the bed, hanging from the ceiling. No matter what position you assumed on the bed, your full form was reflected in the overhead mirror. Striker took out a small leather bag and threw it onto the oak dresser. The tinkling of ice against the side of a glass caused him to turn around and appraise his guest. Her complexion was coal black. Morrine was a big woman, beautifully proportioned. Her breasts swelled the white cupped bra, the top of her powerful thighs peeked out from the sparkling stockings. She smiled and handed him the drink. "You like?" she asked, turning around so that he could get a good look at her buttocks protruding from the white bikini panties.

"Where are your heels"? he asked.

"Oh, they're in the other room. You want me to put them on?" she asked. Her pearly white teeth shone against her bright red lipstick.

"Yeah, go put them on. I got a little candy for you. Go on and cook it up and get you a hit. I definitely got something for you to do."

Morrine came back into the room and spun around in her high heels giving him another view of her hips. "I got some phone calls to make. You can use the kitchen to cook the shit up. I'll call you when I'm ready for you."

She advanced toward him so that her breasts were digging into his chest. Morrine kissed him full on the lips and ground her hips into him. Striker, being totally naked under his silk robe, gripped her hips and slipped his tongue into her mouth. Their lips parted with a loud plop. As she turned, Striker smacked her buttocks with his open hand. Morrine laughed, ran around him and retrieved the leather bag from the bed. She walked sensuously into the next room. Striker caressed the head of his penis, which was erect.

"Hey Low Down, this is Striker," he said.

"Like I don't know your voice. What is it, man?" Low Down replied impatiently.

"Did you take care of our little business?" Striker asked.

"Yeah, the boys took care of it last night." He paused, then said. "Look man, I'm not going to touch the dancer now but the other bitch is fair game as far as I'm concerned."

"Well, your boys sure made a mess of that little adventure. I say, for your sake, let that be for now. Like I told you, this bitch Thelma thinks she is so slick. I'm going to work the hell out of her, then she's all yours. But until then, Low Down, nothing, and I mean nothing, is going to happen to her. I don't even want the girl nervous. It might affect her dancing. After all, she is an artist," he said with contempt.

"I need that cash tonight, Striker," Low Down stated, after a pause.

"Meet me at Hustlers Delight after twelve midnight tonight and you'll be extremely pleased with our new business venture," Striker replied.

"Yeah, later," was Low Down's curt retort. The receiver went dead.

"Hey Baby, you all ready?" Striker yelled out the bedroom doorway.

Still scantily clad, Morrine entered, carrying a glass pipe and a handful of white rocks. "Where can I put these?" she asked referring to the pellets of cocaine.

"Put them on the table beside the bed. Don't worry, it's marble. The surface is as hard as glass."

"Where do you think I've been all my life that I don't know what marble is?" Morrine retorted. "I'm going to get me a hit. Do you mind?" she asked coyly.

"The lighter is in the first drawer on the left," he answered, referring to the night table beside the large circular bed.

Morrine placed one knee on the bed. She tilted the pipe and began drawing the grey smoke into her lungs. Striker came up behind her and tugged the fat part of her hips, then ground his erection into her. He cupped her breasts, one in each hand, and slowly pulled and tweaked her nipples. She, in turn, churned her hips into his penis.

"Don't take too much until you know how good it is," he warned.

Morrine was holding her breath and nodded her head before expelling the smoke. She relaxed her body against his. "Yeah that is good Striker," she said, smiling.

He walked over to his closet and opened the doors outward. On the inside of the doors, were floor-length mirrors. He pulled a latch and let out a mirror of equal length facing him.

"Morrine, get a pillow and come here," he ordered, shrugging off his robe. His penis, fully erect, pointed straight out.

Morrine came around to stand facing him with the pillow dangling from her left hand. Striker grabbed her by her hair and pulled her onto him, kissing her hard. She dropped the pillow at their feet and ground into him. Sliding his hand on the inside of her panties from the rear, he fondled both hips and pushed his erection against her.

Suddenly, he jerked her away from him by grabbing her hair. He directed her downward onto her knees. Striker watched her suck his member in and out of her luscious mouth in the three-way mirrors. He moved his hips backward causing his penis to plop out of her mouth wetly.

"Get another hit, Baby. You got a lot more work to do before your day's over," he snarled. Morrine stumbled up from her kneeling position and retrieved the glass pipe and lighter. She took a bigger hit this time, arranging the small white ball carefully in the pipe. Morrine inhaled deeply and held her breath as long as she dared. *Yes*, she thought. Positioning herself in the three-way mirror, Morrine slowly sank to her knees. She engulfed Striker's member and began sucking again vigorously. Just before he came to a shattering orgasm, Striker cried out Morrine's name. She continued sucking softly well after he was spent. Striker collapsed on the bed and lay spread eagle.

Morrine came from the bath room and peeled her panties to her knees. "I'm a going to get you up again, Striker, I'm hot as hell. You going to screw me?" she asked, throwing her panties to the floor.

"If you do your job, I'll certainly do mine," he replied, as he watched the reflection of her nude form in the overhead mirror climb into bed with him. He sealed a kiss on her lips and rolled over on top of her, losing himself in her soft, satiny flesh.

Across town, Low Down sat in his front room watching the streets come to life with the coming darkness. He picked up a pair of binoculars and scanned the lot across the street. There he is. The nerve of that young punk. This was one of the young men that was supposed to be dead. How he got away from his crew he didn't know, but if he was stupid enough to stay around, he'd have it done if he had to do it himself. He carefully scanned the area behind and in front of the tall, athletic looking youth. He had on a brand new pair of gym shoes. They were the careless generation, who died a dozen a minute and there were a hundred more to take their places. Even Low Down could not figure out the new generation of players. The young Black men of these times seemed not to want to stand out as individuals; they seemed to be overly anxious to please the status quo. It was almost more important to them to seem to be tough than actually be tough. Low Down had to admit a select few of them had real heart. Maybe more heart than he had in his youth. Mutha's ain't got no sense and no concept of loyalty, especially when money started to roll. He shook his head. Hell, who was he to try to solve the problems of our wayward youth. Low Down replaced the binoculars on the table and picked up the ringing phone.

"Who dis?" he greeted. "Turtle, you know who this is. Yeah, well something that you missed is standing across the street in that vacant lot." He paused and frowned. "Fuck all that, he got to go to the store. Shit, you niggas

got a job unfinished. Get y'all asses up and do your job."
Low Down smiled, "Naw, don't come over here, dumb ass.
Just finish your job and I'll call you in a couple of days."
He cradled the phone against his chest before placing it
carefully onto the receiver.

The young man standing across the street was Christopher Rhoreing. The last name was pronounced like the
roar of a lion. That's how Christopher got his nick name,
'The Lion', from his schoolmates in grade school. Conditions at home had been close to normal until his mother's
breakup with his live-in, adopted stepfather of twelve
years. He had never really known his biological father but
had formed a trusting relationship with his stepfather.
Christopher had become angry and bitter, first toward his
stepfather, then at his mother. His mother had taken to
guys just a little older then him. This had caused him
considerable mental anguish. Instead of going to football
practice, where he had solidified a football scholarship for
his play as a defensive back, he had taken to the streets.
His family of unconditional love and acceptance had come
from a street gang called the Scorpios, but with a price.

Little did Low Down or any of his henchmen know that
Jamal was Christopher's first cousin. Lion had come to
lure Low Down, himself, out of his house to take revenge
on his cousin and his cut partners who Low Down had
ordered hit. When the murders of the bloods, who had
taken over Low Down's reefer business, had taken place,
Lion had been snuggled up with a honey named Zelda
across town. Her sex was so good, he had missed the
gang's weekly meeting. It was then and there that Low
Down's men had struck. Lion, coming home on the subway, had run into one of the neighborhood homies who
informed him about his cousin, Jamal, and his gang mem-

bers. Lion had gone to his secret stash and upgraded from a snub nose thirty-eight revolver to a fifteen shot nine millimeter automatic. He had five full clips in each pocket, totalling ten clips. Lion was one of those few young men with a lot of heart and loyalty, even to those dead.

A flash of light from the window across the street caught his attention. Lion ducked around the corner of a torn out wall. He took out his binoculars and surveyed the window. Yeah, there that muthafucka was, watching him. Wonder if he knows that I'm watching him too. Well, if ol' Low Down had spotted him, either he would come out himself or send somebody. On the opposite side of the empty lot stood a row of boarded up houses. It was these houses Lion planned to use to effect his getaway, maybe taking a couple of people out before he left.

Lion walked across what he thought would be Low Down's line of vision. This was to make sure that Low Down knew he was still around. He pulled out his automatic and checked to make sure that a round was in the chamber. All he would have to do is flip the safety and he'd be on.

A yellow Cadillac slowly rolled up the street. Originally, Lion had planned to lure them into the vacant building across the street and ambush the gunmen there. Seeing the yellow Caddy rolling up the street, Lion did what lions do best. He attacked. Aw, what the hell, he thought, pulling his weapon and running toward the car. Hunters usually did not expect to be hunted, and Turtle riding shotgun did not expect to be killed so unceremoniously, without even a hello. The first round shattered the window and tore half his face off. Turtle slumped forward, dead without a shudder. Scoot veered the car sharply away from the gunman and stomped the gas pedal to the floor. The automobile burned rubber, careening down the street.

Lion, seeing that it was useless to give chase, pivoted like he was on the football field chasing down a receiver and headed for the abandoned rowhouses, arms and legs pumping.

Scoot, meanwhile, had spun the automobile into a U-turn and was headed back toward the vacant lot. Little Mack jumped out at the curb and proceeded at a cautious trot toward the rowhouses. The yellow Caddy sped around the block to stop midway in the street. Lion, breathing freely, waited in a basement, watching his pursuers from a window that was just above ground level. Little Mack was watching the windows above ground level and didn't look in Lion's direction. Scoot walked slowly up the side-walk looking in both directions. He motioned with the barrel of his pistol for Little Mack to get back into the car. Both men backed away from the building, got into the car and slowly pulled away. Lion, not easily fooled, waited a half hour before leaving the vacated building. Yeah, muthafucka's one down, and three to go, he bragged to himself. He hurried to his car. He'd be over Zelda's to-night.

Low Down had watched the entire sequence of events from his upstairs window. He could not believe that a young punk like that could take out one of his boys and go unpunished. When he spied the youth run into the vacant building, he was tempted to go after him. But, the youth's recklessness frightened him. Shit, I must be getting old, he reflected to himself. This calls for someone a little bit better, the city's finest. It would be fitting that a police-man should kill this young upstart. He reached for the phone, "Let me speak to Lieutenant Flippo."

"Yes, Lieutenant Flippo speaking," Flippo answered, chewing on one of his smelly sandwiches.

"This is Low Down, Flippo. I got a little problem that I need for you to take care of," Low Down stated smoothly.

"I told you never to call me here," Flippo whispered tensely. He dropped his sandwich in his attempt to cup the receiver.

Low Down laughed softly. "Don't worry, Flippo. It's the first and only time. This problem's named Lion. You know the kid that I spoke to you about a couple of days ago?"

"What's his real name? I don't know why you people don't use the names your parents gave you," Flippo stated, while fumbling around on his desk for a pen. "Christopher Rhoreing. OK, I got it. I'll talk to you tomorrow night." Flippo did not wait for a response, he quickly hung up the phone.

Thelma, standing off stage, rocked her shoulders
and hips to a recent rap tune. She had added it to her act
because of its funky bass and drum line. Slowly placing
one foot in front of the other, she fan danced to center
stage. Her costume consisted of mesh, skintight black
pants, a black turtleneck tank top, and black pumps.
Turning her back to the audience, Thelma fan danced a
little deeper by undulating her hips and letting her hands
push her thighs. The tempo changed from a slow funk to a
hot, up-tempo tune slinging lyrics directly from the
streets of urban America. This was Jackie's cue. Unlike
Thelma, she came on stage in a blur — bumping, and
whirling in silver pumps, black biker shorts, and a purple
spandex top. The two danced opposite each other, each
commanding the extreme edges of the stage. Thelma took
center stage, slipped gracefully out her pants, and picked
up the intensity. She spun off stage. Then, it was Jackie's
turn to dance solo. At the conclusion of the performance,
both women came out and bowed with their backs to the
audience. The applause was deafening.

"I told you they would like that number," Thelma said.
She turned to look upward at Jackie, who was following
her down the steep staircase to their backstage dressing
room.

"Yeah, that was hot. Where did you learn how to choreo-
graph like that?" Jackie asked.

Thelma shut the dressing room door firmly behind her.
She turned and said, "I learned it by watching other

dancers. I know what looks good to the eye and what doesn't. I took modern dance when I was a young bopper and my instructor always encouraged me to pursue choreography."

Thelma began peeling the few remaining garments from her body. "Whew, I really sweated this outfit out," she said, turning to Jackie and dangling the threads in front of her.

Jackie was suddenly upon her, pressing her naked body onto Thelma's. Thelma returned the wet hot kiss instinctively before pushing Jackie roughly away. Flashbacks of her dancing instructor invaded her consciousness.

"Don't ever do that again, Jackie," Thelma shouted, holding her hands out in front of her. The two women stood sweating and panting from the brief exertion.

"Hey, I'm sorry, Thelma. I just been wanting to get with you for sometime. Morrine said that you was game," Jackie added, trying to justify her attempt to seduce Thelma.

Thelma's eyes narrowed. She remembered Morrine's hand high up on her thigh. "Morrine lied ,Jackie, but, whether you believe her or not, is not the issue. Don't ever touch me like that again," she stated, her eyes flashing.

"Look, we've been friends for the last six months. I made a mistake. I'm sorry, Thelma. It won't happen again," Jackie reiterated.

The tiny dressing room eased off the tension like a steam valve. Adjoining the dressing room, were two showers, which were no more then stalls separated by transparent shower curtains. Thelma could clearly see the outline of Jackie as she showered with her back to her. Thelma dressed in her customary jeans and sweat shirt. Slinging her travel bag over her shoulder, she was on her way out. Thelma stopped and took a look at her dancing partner.

Jackie, dressed in baggy trousers and huge flop hat, resembled a college student. Thelma was still angry but felt sorry for Jackie. All these months, Jackie had never mentioned a family member or, for that matter, anyone in her personal life.

"Hey, we cool. I just ain't in to that," Thelma said, patting Jackie on the back. Jackie was obviously embarrassed, her eyes downcast.

"Just watch your back, Thelma. If you need me for anything on the up and up, beep me," Jackie answered, hesitant to look Thelma in the eye.

Thelma hurried out of the club onto the street. "Cabby, hey cabby," she yelled, hailing down a green and white cab. "Take me to Fourteenth and Lagross Street," she instructed to the dredlocked driver.

It was three in the morning and the streets were deserted. The cab had to slow to a crawl, neither occupant was familiar with the area, and the street numbers were either nonexistent or worn away by the years.

"This is it, 1423 Lagross," Thelma stated.

She paid the cab driver, and, after looking for a buzzer and finding none, knocked on the door. A man built on the same frame as Jason answered the door. He had on a red and black bathrobe, wearing no shirt and a pair of faded jeans.

"You're Bobby, Morrine's brother," Thelma exclaimed.

She caught herself, he smiled and she melted. Stared. That's all Thelma did was stare.

"Oh, Thelma, remember me, I'm Jason." Jason broke the spell. He had been sitting on an old, overstuffed easy chair. While sitting, he was hidden from view.

"Hey, Jason," Thelma greeted. Smiling brightly, she seated herself on the couch and tried not to look at Bobby.

"Can I get you anything, Thelma?" Bobby asked.

"I'd like some juice or water, if it's not too inconvenient," she responded.

"This is what we're going to do," Jason began.

They were all sitting around a small wooden table. Thelma periodically cast her eyes upward toward Bobby. He seemed not to be aware of her attention. However, it was not lost on Jason.

"Thelma, I want you to act as if nothing is happening. Continue to dance and basically keep your regular routine. I'm going to move in with Tiffenie. She don't know it yet, but I don't think it will be a problem. At least until this whole thing is under control." He paused, looked at Thelma, then at Bobby, who always seemed detached.

"You won't have to move in with Jomo," Jason said. "He's involved in some other activities that will keep him out of town for a while. Bobby is there. Anything that you would like to add?"

Bobby returned from his detached state to finally look at Thelma, then at Jason. "Thelma, it's important that you keep Dewvel relaxed. What I mean is that he does not have a clue you have a plan. I'm certain that he plans either to break you down through drugs and prostitution, or outright murder you. Low Down is a problem because we know that Striker and he are business partners, but we don't know if, in fact, Striker has any control over Low Down. Low Down is a treacherous mutha and he might break rank and take you out despite Dewvel's order not to hurt you."

He walked over to the lone dresser in the apartment and, from under some jeans, pulled out a snubnose thirty eight. "I want you to keep this with you all the time," Bobby stated, handing the gun to Thelma.

Thelma reached into her waistband and extracted her Beretta 380. "I won't need that. I have one of my own."

For the first time Bobby's eyes shone a flicker of respect and admiration. Thelma handed her gun to Bobby for his inspection.

"This is a good piece. Have you fired it yet?"

"Yeah, I go to the shooting range out on Parkside at least three times a week. I haven't gone lately because of this mess that I've gotten us in," she added regretfully.

"Don't even go there, sister love. It's not your fault that we live in an economic system that forces us to exploit and murder each other to survive. We have to develop another system within this system that nurtures our life instead of cheapening it," Bobby stated.

"Well, along with this other society, I do believe that women have equal rights. Am I correct, brotherlove?" Thelma asked, her eyebrows arched.

"Yeah, that's correct," replied Bobby.

"Then why in the hell are you Brothers making all of these plans without consulting Tiff or me?" There was a pause, then Thelma continued. "This is ideological trash, especially if you're talkin' 'bout real revolution. If I'm correct, liberation includes all social interactions of the people," she said, standing and slashing her index finger about like a saber. "So that, my Brothers, this means that if the relationship that men have had with women are exploitative, dehumanizing, and unfair, this has to be corrected also."

Jason was stunned. A smile crossed Bobby's lips. "This Sister has had some political education, haven't you, Thelma?"

Thelma smiled an impish grin that Jason had not seen before. He remembered when Tiffenie had been telling him about events related to her by Thelma. He had not paid attention. If Bobby or Sister Clarice had listened to Tiffenie, they would not have missed the fact that Thelma had a certain degree of political development. Something that The Organization was always on the lookout for.

"Who schooled you, Thelma?" Bobby again this time insisting a reply.

"It's a long story, but when I was in the motor city, a guy lived upstairs who read a lot. Supposedly, he was a Nationalist. Through him I learned a lot, since I didn't have anything else to do but dance. I read the books that he gave me. The material that I covered forced me to look at things differently. I just seemed to lose hope. It seemed that the Brothers were never going to take themselves seriously. Just reading and rapping ain't going to get it. It all sounded like a fairy tale until now. I want to know more about this 'Organization,' Bobby."

"For now, you can just do as you're asked and we will keep you informed. I admit, and apologize in the way that we took you for granted, as if you or Tiffenie would not have any valuable input. We were wrong and it won't happen again," Bobby said. His tone and mannerism convinced Thelma that he was sincere.

"Well let's go, Thelma. I'll have to get some sleep before I go into work tomorrow," Jason interrupted.

Bobby and Jason shook hands warmly. She and Bobby shook hands in an offhand manner, one in which she somehow did not care for. Thelma frowned.

"What's the matter with you?" Jason asked, once in the car.

"I did not like the way Bobby shook my hand," she replied.

Jason looked at her out of the corner of his eye and shook his head. Women, they all just crazy, he thought, as they sped through the early morning streets.

It took a while for Thelma to get to sleep; there were so many issues at hand. Number one priority was getting Tiff up to snuff, then whatever move they made, she'd be in shape to go with them. Thelma knew then that she liked Jomo for a friend but who she wanted was Bobby. Jackie had told her to watch her back after telling her that Morrine said she was game. Could she trust Morrine? Well, she'd put her to a test. Tiff gets out of the hospital today. Jason said that he would pick her up on his way to work. They would check out Tiffenie, then Thelma would take Jason's car and take her home. Mercifully, fatigue triumphed. Thelma slept like a rock.

Tiffenie thought Jason looked like he'd been under a lot of stress; his clothes were meticulously ironed, but he looked ruffled. She greeted him at the hospital by giving him a long wet kiss and tonguing him right in front of Thelma and the nurse. Jason could not believe Tiffenie; she acted like nothing significant had taken place and they were about to go home to a white, picket-fenced dream home. He gently pushed her away by placing his hand on her stomach.

"You missed me?" she asked.

"Yeah, you know I did, but quit it," Jason whispered.

He suddenly had a rock hard erection. Tiffenie looked at his crotch and giggled. Thelma, with a disgusted scowl on her face, said, "I'm ready to get out of here."

Once in the car, Jason turned to Tiffenie and said, "Look girl, quit it. I got to go to work." Thelma in the back seat could tell by the position of Tiff's shoulder and arm that she had her hand somewhere in Jason's crotch. He was squirming.

"I thought you would at least take today off," Tiffenie said pouting.

"No, I got to go to work, Tiffenie," he stated, sweat glistening on his forehead.

"You comin' over tonight?" Tiffenie asked, smiling broadly. Jason had a difficult time extracting himself from the car.

"Yeah, I'll be over tonight," he answered, walking awkwardly up the steps to the Pear Building.

Thelma buckled her seat beat and eased the car into the morning traffic. She drove carefully, taking the streets instead of the highway. The traffic this time of the morning was a killer.

"So, you and Jason havin' sex?" Thelma asked.

"Naw, we role playing," Tiffenie replied, keeping a straight face. Both women broke out laughing.

"Tiff, you going to have to get serious. We in some deep stuff and, all of a sudden, you Ms. Horny."

Thelma began concentrating on driving. Tiffenie leaned back in her seat and expelled a breath of air and said, "All of a sudden, Thelma I'm alive. The air smells different, I feel things that I haven't felt in years. I can be naughty with Jason and I know that he really cares for me. I have a real friend that cares about me and accepts me. This is what living is all about — people that mean something to you. I don't care what we do. I don't care about my stupid job. I just care about life and the people who give it meaning."

"Well look here, Miss Mary Poppins, if we swimming in the river with concrete around our feet, I don't think that you'll have that same cheery outlook," Thelma replied sweetly.

"They wouldn't dare try that again. The policemen are investigating the case as we speak," Tiffenie stated.

"Tiff, I don't know what I'm going to have to do to give you a dose of reality. Organized crime cannot function without the cooperation of the police. And we, my dear friend, are dealing with organized crime folks. So the final analysis is that the police might be as dangerous to us as Low Down or Striker."

Just mentioning his name caused cold chills to run down her spine. She must have shivered outwardly because Tiffenie asked if she was cold. Thelma circled the block twice before stopping before Tiff's apartment. She was being extra careful. Tiff acted like she did not have a care in the world. It must be love, Thelma thought.

"Tiff how do you feel," Thelma asked, once seated comfortably in Tiffenie's apartment.

"I'm still a little bit sore, and my jaw hurts where that guy socked me, but I'm OK," Tiffenie answered.

"I'm going home and going back to bed. I'd advise you to get your rest. You gave us all a scare," Thelma added.

"I'm happy to get out of that cold ass hospital. It's a wonder that I don't have pneumonia," Tiffenie said.

"When are you going back to work?"

"I'm going tomorrow. I told my boss that I had been in a slight automobile accident," Tiffenie explained.

"In a couple of weeks I'll have about eight grand saved. How are you on the money?"

"I got my ten grand in a permanent account and I got about four grand saved in my junk account," Tiffenie answered.

"Girl, what you doing with all that money?" Thelma asked, her eyebrows arched.

"All I been doing is working and saving. I got the ten grand from a will that my uncle left when he died. I don't own a car; all I do is buy clothes and furniture."

"Well, I don't know about the fellows but I got to have cash. There is no telling where we'll be in the next couple of weeks," Thelma stated.

Tiffenie walked Thelma to the door and gave her a hug. Once on the sidewalk, Thelma almost went to catch a cab before remembering that she had Jason's car. This meeting that had been arranged by Bobby for her to meet this Mrs. C. worried her, but she was not afraid. Maybe she could begin to put some of the pieces to the puzzle together. Thelma would meet with this Mrs. C., or who ever she was, around seven.

Patricia Clarice was patron and head usher of Big Hope Baptist Church. She was also head of intelligence for the 'Organization.' All the recent big robberies had been planned and sanctioned by her. Recently, there had been a power struggle within the organization. Miss Clarice was now in charge of both divisions of intelligence. She had ordered a surveillance team to watch Thelma and she had sacrificed her valuable time to do some record searches on her. Miss Clarice gathered information on people to control them. This Thelma girl got turned around; something happened in her life. If anyone could find out what, Miss Clarice could.

Miss Clarice would do anything for the 'Organization.' It was her church personified. She believed in the old time religion's *'smite your enemies to dust lest they betray the righteous cause.'* Clarice enjoyed her faceless existence. Anyone not knowing the depth of what they saw would see a simple old woman.

Frequently, she would visit Hustlers Delight during happy hour. The waitress would show her directly to her table, positioned against the far corner. From this position, one could watch everyone coming in or out and be hidden by the shadows. Her real power came from her knowledge of what went on in the city and who were the minor and major players, legal or not. After a certain dollar amount, it didn't matter; money came to money dirty or clean.

This young man, so appropriately named 'Lion', was her immediate concern. She felt certain that, if she could have this young man brought to her all in one piece, she could turn him to their way of thinking. Just think, a young lion to nurture and turn to The Organization — this is what she lived for. Thelma was a likely candidate. However, she might prove to be a liability. That could be tragic for Thelma, but was not all her children's lives tragic? Yes, it was better to die, if one must, for The Organization, then to just die. This was Sister C's philosophy on life and death. Within The Organization, in extremely quiet whispers among those who you would only trust with your life, she was labeled 'Sister Death'.

"I'd like my usual," she stated curtly to the scantily dressed waitress. As was her habit, when waiting, she beat a rhythmic tune with her fingers upon the table. Today, she was dressed in her old frock flower dress, flop cotton hat and black granny boots that were laced almost to the knee. Miss Clarice had taken off her square, dark granny glasses upon entering the club. When her drink arrived, she had it sent back, for it was not to her taste.

Bobby arrived just after six. She watched him as he entered and greeted the patrons. Bobby was very popular in more than one circle of friends.

"Greeting's, Sister Clarice," Bobby stated, sliding into the seat across from her.

She clasped his hand in both of hers and held him there. He met her steady gaze with one of his own. Sister Clarice released his hand when her drink arrived the second time. She sipped it and nodded her head to the waiting waitress.

"What news do you have of this young Lion?" she asked.

"We know where he is, but there are others who wish to find him besides Low Down. Our sources tell us that the police are looking for him high and low. Informants on the streets have told us that there is a reward for the knowledge of his whereabouts. We're certain that Low Down has joined with the police to hunt down and kill this young Lion."

Bobby paused to order a 7-Up. He watched Sister C. carefully, for he also feared her. "What does it matter if he is killed or not. He is of the generation that has no beginning or end. What use will he be for us?" Bobby asked.

"He will be used as a weapon to further our cause. If he proves to be a liability, we'll kill him ourselves, but he might be worth some investment of time, education and materials. When this chore is finished, he might be reeducated to go into another city and bring us others like himself. Young, swift of feet and mind, and fearless," she said, leaning back into her chair and taking a sip of her drink, her eyes never leaving Bobby's.

"What would you have me do, Sister Clarice?"

"If at all possible, bring him to me all in one piece, and see if I can turn him. He has killed one of our enemies. Maybe, with our assistance, he can kill them all," she replied.

"So it is said, so it will be done," Bobby answered, keeping his voice barely above a whisper. This response was protocol when a direct order was given from a superior of The Organization.

"Have you any more information on this Thelma?" she asked, watching him closely.

Bobby aware of his emotions maintained a blank expression. "She has a solid foundation of political education. It is not clear what her level of development is. However, I plan to get her involved in our Literacy Program and our Young Mother's Social Circle. From her interaction with these programs, we'll know soon enough on what level, if any, we can utilize her," Bobby stated, trying very hard to keep his voice neutral.

Sister Clarice crossed her legs and seemed to lose interest, just for a moment, in the conversation at hand. "Do you desire this woman?" she asked, suddenly trying to catch Bobby off guard.

He hesitated. This was all she needed for an answer. She held her hand outward, quieting him. "Women like her can be a great service to The Organization, or, like the other side of a coin, can be just as detrimental. Wiggling her ass for money... Maybe we can get her to wiggle that ass for the 'Organization.' What do you say to that Bobby?" she asked, her tone brutal.

"Like you have told me many times before, the waters are not yet tested. Until we know its depth, who can say," he answered.

She laughed, suddenly covering her mouth with her hand. "Ah, you young men and your lust. It makes you idiots more times then not. I know you, Bobby, almost as well as anyone. This women, is she loose of morals, does she sleep with anyone who has a piece of rock or fifty dollars to throw away?" She did not wait for a answer. "You like this woman, Bobby, but I don't condemn you for it. She is attractive and seems to have some depth to her. You did not ask permission for the Central Crew to place her in these programs, which is uncharacteristic of you. It is good, for you have not shown any interest in a woman except for lust in a long time. Beat her if you have to. Dominate her. Force her to give you sons if she's capable, but don't forget that your first and last love is The Organization," she stated evenly.

Downing the last vestiges of liquid from her tall glass, she looked around for the waitress to order another. Bobby was forever amazed at her ability to know what you were thinking before you were sure what your thoughts were. It was true he was attracted to Thelma, but he had not even admitted it to himself. Sister Clarice had picked up on it immediately. Maybe he just wanted to sex her, but no he had to be honest with himself; she'd be a good companion or mate, but could he trust her? His thoughts were cut short.

"There is another matter that we must discuss," she began. Their conversation was interrupted. The waitress was new and tried to get Sister Clarice to pay for her drinks. "I don't pay anything here, young girl. Go talk to someone who knows who I am and next time, don't be so impertinent." The waitress rolled her eyes at Sister Clarice and disappeared to somewhere in the back. "These young people, it's no wonder they don't live past the age of eighteen," she admonished.

Leaning forward she said, "Your sister is smoking again and has been seen with Striker on more than one occasion. It would be unfortunate if she divulged any information about us to him. Does she know anything?"

She had leaned forward; he could feel her breath on his face. This was serious; it could mean his sister's life.

"All she knows is that I'm part of an Organization of Black people, who want to improve the quality of life for our people. She knows nothing of what we do, at least I haven't told her anything," Bobby answered, keeping his facial expression as blank as possible.

"We've all made monumental sacrifices to get to where we are and the ante has gone up, Bobby. I love you, and I know that you love your sister very much. It don't mean a thang if any of our emotions should spoil our judgement. Handle it anyway that you can, but when the time is right, you'd better see that she is not anywhere near him." She paused and took a sip of her drink. "Now let's get down to the logistics of this operation."

Sister Clarice extracted a brown manila folder from beneath the table. She took out a clip board and a pen. "Here's the deal Bobby, our connections in the police department pinpoint a Lieutenant Flippo as a dirty cop. He works for Striker. We won't ever have to worry about him, but this Captain Shultz is causing problems. We had planned to launder our money through our people in Nigeria. There is a hold up. We feel that the international intelligence community has a feel that something big is operating. We've kept pretty much undercover, but now we're feeling pressure. Our programs are being monitored by the police department in this city. A couple of our informants have turned up missing and our science program in Ghana is under scrutiny from the U.S., Canada, and Great Britain. You see, niggas ain't supposed to have money and we're definitely not supposed to finance science programs overseas. Especially ones that the western powers don't have any say over.

"So, even though we've been very careful not to draw attention to ourselves, the growth and development of the organization has everyone looking. We have twenty million dollars that we have to launder. It's crucial that we clean these resources for the next phase of our operation. This is where Striker comes in. You see, unknown to him and his bank buddies downtown, they clean our money when they clean his. Our agent downtown is the go-between. When Dewvels and his covert money is laundered, so is ours. Our money is 'just' money. As revolutionaries, we know that all wealth around us is ours. It's a matter of securing it in one fashion or another. Someone downtown picked up on the discrepancies. Silvia is under a lot of scrutiny from this Captain Shultz. She is our most valuable agent. This Captain Shultz sees a relationship. We have decided to become proactive and distort the picture by killing Dewvel and Low Down. This will make it look like a war between Low Down and Dewvel. That's why it's important that you and Jason carry out the job and make it look like a gang war. Any type of weapons that you'll need, we'll furnish to you." She paused and toyed with her empty glass. "Are there any questions?" she asked.

"Miller explained to us that we would have to leave town after the job was over. Where will we go and what assignment will The Organization give us?"

"You will go to Houston and organize just like you've done here. You'll be given two hundred thousand dollars cash upon completing the job and a car will be provided to you. The decision that you'll have to make is to determine who in your party is unwanted baggage and eliminate them. Don't go soft on me, Bobby. If Thelma or this petty bourgeoisie girl, Tiffenie, prove to be a hindrance or a security risk, they will have to be dealt with. If you don't have the nerve to do your job, tell me now; I'll have someone do what you can't or won't do."

She looked at her watch. "Thelma is to meet me here in the next ten minutes. Stay until she gets here. Make her feel comfortable with me, which I don't think will be a problem because I've meet her before. Then you go and get this lion cub for me. Is that understood?"

Bobby nodded his head and turned to see Thelma enter the club. Bobby and Miss Clarice watched Thelma scan the club and make a beeline toward their table.

"Hi, Bobby," Thelma greeted. This corner of the club was always in the shadows and it took her eyes a moment to adjust to the gloom. "Miss Clarice, is that you?" Thelma began leaning forward and squinting at the figure in the corner.

"Yes, child, it's me. Have a seat," she replied, her tone slightly chilly.

Thelma, sensitive to vibes, felt the chill and, in turn, sat between the two and fell silent.

"Would you like anything to drink?" Bobby asked.

"Yeah, some 7-Up would be fine," she answered. Thelma noticed Miss Clarice sitting in Hustlers Delight like she owned the place. Maybe some of the pieces to this puzzle would fall together today, Thelma thought. She was tingling all over. Thelma waited for Miss Clarice This was obviously her show. She looked up and was drawn into the dark brown eyes of Clarice.

"I had a feeling that I would see you again, Thelma," Clarice began.

"Me too," Thelma replied.

"Bobby, you can go." Miss Clarice waved Bobby away.

"I'll pick Thelma up in a hour and a half," he stated, rising to leave. Their eyes meet, though only briefly. Thelma sighed, Miss Clarice smiled.

"I have only this to tell you," she began leaning forward, as was her manner. "You're in a lot of danger, but, many times in life, successful men and women take adverse situations and turn them into a plus. Your last performance is two weeks and a couple days from this date. After your performance, you are to leave directly from the stage to the side door. A car will be waiting for you there. You'll not see this city again. Bobby will show you where to get another set of identification papers."

Sister Clarice paused and looked at Thelma's face carefully. "A wig, some makeup, and we can make you look like another person," she added.

"What's this all about, Sister Clarice? It's obvious that you're of some rank within this organization, but what concern does this organization have with an exotic dancer?"

"Simply this. Your little escapade with Low Down has given us a reason to eliminate him and cover our trail. I'm sorry I can't tell you more. However, Bobby has pointed out that you do have some ideological development. You might consider joining us, but I'll warn you, this Organization exacts a heavy price. You no longer belong to yourself, you belong to The Organization. Where you live, the type of work that you do, sometimes who you might have an affair with, is determined by the needs of The Organization." She patted Thelma's hand, which was folded on the table. "You're free to involve yourself with our community programs. That way you'll be able to get a detailed look at The Organization and we'll get a chance to get a good look at you."

"Why is everything so secretive? I think that the Literacy Program is something that we've needed for some time. Why would you have to veil it along with the other programs that you have?" Thelma asked.

"I really don't have the time or the authority to tell you all of that, Thelma. Watch what goes on around you and, if you're in doubt, tell Bobby. Here he is, anyway."

Bobby had entered and stood by the door waiting for Thelma. At the doorway, Thelma turned to wave good-bye to Miss Clarice but she had disappeared.

THOSE WHO STRADDLE THE FENCE SOON ARE SPLIT IN TWO

Captain Shultz laid the report carefully on his desk. The Federal Government had a sudden interest in these robberies, and had informed him that his department was under some type of investigation. Every phrase of the investigation was super hush hush. He was about to walk to the window and look out into the alley when the phone caused him to return to his desk.

"Hello. Yes, this is Captain Shultz. So you think that you've identified the person responsible for interfacing the extra funds. Yes, I'll be available this afternoon."

Shultz hung up the phone and sat with his head in his hands. Something was amiss, and it led to this precinct. Well, the meeting this morning with the Federal agents should give him more information than he had now. Shultz looked at his watch. His morning meeting was in a hour. He called Flippo but could not get a hold of him. That's strange, he thought. Flippo knew the circumstances and he had strict orders to be available twenty-four hours.

Flippo had deliberately turned off his beeper. He sat directly across the street with two other men from an apartment that this Lion was supposed to be holed up in. Flippo turned to the larger of the two men.

"Get ready if he's here. We want to end this thing as quickly as possible."

The man nodded and slung the rifle with the large zoom scope onto his shoulder and sighted the weapon on the second floor window across the street. The outline of a figure could be seen on the drawn shade.

"Pour me a drink, honey," said Zelda.

She did nothing to hide her nakedness. Her cone-shaped breasts wiggled as she walked across the room to receive the drink from Lion. He pulled her onto his lap and nuzzled her breasts with his nose and mouth. Zelda attempted to put a passion mark on Lion's neck. Roughly he pushed her away.

"Hey I ain't on all that," he stated, standing and knocking her off his lap.

"I told you about being so rough with me, Lion," said Zelda, pushing him in the chest with both hands.

Laughing, he stumbled slightly and pulled her to him.

"What are you going to do, now," she asked.

"I'm going to hang out here for a day or two, then I'm going to change up. Goin' to hide out somewhere in the downtown area. They won't expect me to be down there," he added.

He fondled her derrière and softly bit her lower lip. Zelda unbuckled his belt. He was barefoot and shirtless. Lion carelessly threw his jeans to the floor and led her by the hand to the bed located against the far wall. He positioned her on her hands and knees and entered her from behind. Zelda grunted as he picked up the tempo of their lovemaking. Lion's mind swirled as their passion reached the predictable conclusion.

"Oh yeah, somebody asked about you, but it wasn't the police. It was that guy that's always passing out that militant literature," Zelda said. They were lying in bed snuggled tightly against each other.

Lion sat upright in bed. "Why didn't you tell me?" he asked, agitated.

"I didn't tell him anything. I just told him that I hadn't seen you in a while."

"We just started messing around last week. How would they know that you even knew me," he asked more to himself.

"The only person that knows I'm seeing you is Shaunda, my sister," she answered, innocently. Lion fell silent.

"I got to get out of here," he stated. Lion dressed quickly. Pulling a duffle bag from under the kitchen table, he pulled out his nine and made sure that he had a round in the chamber. He clicked the magazine back into the gun and began throwing his scant possessions into the duffle bag. Zelda donned a fluffy, yellow terrycloth robe. She draped her arms around his shoulders.

"Who you know downtown? Another girl?"

"Baby, you don't understand. People are trying to kill me. The fact that someone asked you about me means that somebody knows that I'm in this area. I got to get out of here," he stated, exasperation in his voice.

Lion peeped out the window, pulling the shade slightly to one side.

"Lion," she called his name. At the moment that he turned his head to look in her direction, a loud pop, along with the sound of breaking glass, resounded in the apartment.

"Get down, Zelda!" he shouted.

She stood and ran toward him. Another pop splashed a deep red splotch in her chest. Her body was thrown to the floor, twitched once and was still. He knew she was dead without going to the corpse. Lion stuck the pistol in his waist band, snatched his bag and ran out of the door. Instead of going out the front, he went to the hall window that over looked the fire escape. Breaking the glass with his duffle bag, Lion climbed out through the window onto the landing. He jumped the last eight feet to the alley and kicked in his world-class sprinter speed, the bag bouncing against his shoulder.

Three blocks later, looking to his right then to his left, he slowed to a walk. Ducking into a doorway, he scanned the streets behind him. Bending, he unzipped his duffle bag and retrieved the ten clips, a flashlight and a small pair of binoculars. Ditching the bag, Lion sauntered back onto the street. Three men one of whom he was vaguely familiar with were walking toward him. The man, who he had seen in his 'hood, looked directly at him. Lion attempted to pull his weapon. It was too late — all three men had pistols pointed at his chest.

"Lion, I think that you'd better come with us," the taller of the men stated.

He was escorted down a side street and into a waiting car. Sandwiched in the back seat between the men, the man named Raffiki turned around in his seat and said, "Man, you're fast. You almost killed us old men trying to keep up with you." The manner of his voice did not sound like one that was about to take a life.

"What do you muthas want with me," Lion asked.

"Someone wants to see you, young man. In your predicament, I wouldn't ask too many questions. After it's all said and done, you still breathing, nigga," Raffiki added.

The eyes of a woman met his in the rearview mirror. She looked familiar. "I'm Shaunda, Zelda's sister, Lion."

"Well, hope you got a black dress, 'cause y'all going to a funeral. Your sister's dead," he stated. Her eyes clouded. Lion, unperturbed, looked out the window.

Back at the police station, Shultz tried to keep his face devoid of emotion, but to no avail. He was blushing from his neck up. The evidence was solid, his best friend and partner were working for the scum of the city. All together, six agents had come from Washington D.C. Not only had they revealed to him that Flippo was receiving a large stipend for allowing graft, drugs, and prostitution, but there was feasible evidence that he was involved in at least four murders in the last two years.

"What do you propose that we do?" Shultz asked, his voice wavering.

Wearing a cutaway navy blue suit, white shirt and blue tie, Agent Brown rose from the conference table and walked to the chalk board. His face was pockmarked and he had a wide mouth with nonexistent lips. Blue eyes sparkling, he said, "We're going to use this, Lieutenant Flippo. We're not overly upset that he works for one of the biggest organized crime families in this part of the country. Dirty cops help the economy, if you know what I mean. What we are worried about is this Nigerian connection. At first, we thought that it was another money laundering scheme. We have uncovered an organization in this city that seeks to upset the delicate balance of power in this country. They have money, a research center in Ghana, and we suspect they have infiltrated positions, not only in this country, but the continent of Africa, as well as the Caribbean Islands. At this time, we're not sure if Flippo's connected or not, but we can use his position to get closer then we are now."

"How do you propose to do that?" Shultz asked.

"We'll know more after we speak with Lieutenant Flippo. Would you get him in here, Shultz?"

"I've tried to contact him. He disappeared this morning. I left a message with his secretary to see me as soon as he gets in," Shultz answered.

"I don't give a fuck if you have to go find him yourself. Have him here by 14 hundred hours," Brown stated sharply, his blue eyes burning a hole into Shultz.

"I thought you were one of the best," Flippo said to the man with the high powered rifle.

"If that stupid broad hadn't got in the way, he'd be dead," the man responded.

"Let's pack it up, fellows. I have to get down to the station," Flippo ordered.

He was pissed. This means that he would have to talk to Low Down face to face. Since becoming indebted to Striker, Flippo had seen the other side of life. Everything and everyone had a price. A simple loan had turned him into a dirty cop. Of course, there were perks that went along with the job. Women, the best liquor and his salary tripled. Both of his daughters went to an Ivy League school in upstate New York. Soon he'd have enough saved to retire from the police department and live the good life. His ex-wife had died suddenly in an automobile accident. The accident had been facilitated by Low Down. At least he wouldn't have to worry about paying alimony. Every once in a while, he felt a pang of guilt, but he remembered what she sent him through. The scorn of a woman... he knew the score. The bitch was dead and good for her and him. Once back in his office, his secretary informed him that the Captain was anxious to see him. Flippo went into his office to clean up some paperwork. He looked up, and there stood Captain Shultz. The expression on his face caused Flippo's stomach to turn sour.

"Yeah, Captain, I got word from my secretary. I was on my way up to see you," Flippo said, rising from his chair.

"Don't get up, Flippo. I want you in the conference room at Two P.M. sharp," Shultz hissed.

"What's wrong, Captain? You look like you've seen a ghost."

"After this conference meeting, we'll see who sees ghosts," Shultz responded.

He turned on his heel and walked out of the office. Flippo sat stunned. His skin turned icy cold. He glanced at his watch. No, it would be stupid to try to contact Striker, at least not now. His mind raced ahead to fathom the many possibilities that lay in wait for him in this conference. The fact that his career was in jeopardy was moot, this could mean his life.

At that moment, in a downtown business complex, Silvia, clad in a two-piece tweed suit, tried to merge her body with the wall. Security guards strolled past, looking into every corner.

"I got to get out of here!" she said to herself, just as they passed.

Silvia Burnice Williams was Senior Executive of BroudSum Bank, with a Masters Degree in Finance from Cornell University. She took only six years to make Senior Manager. Silvia was beautiful, articulate, and when necessary, personable. Add this to seasoned knowledge and understanding of the business of banking, and you got professionalism personified. Upon graduation, Silvia had illusions of the grandeur of international banking. After her first four years, she realized that it was an example of the worst type of greed and corruption, all cloaked in the name of free enterprise. It was no longer an issue of nations, states, and independent countries. It was the decisions of multinational companies that beat to the tune of famine, economic ruin, and war. Whether it be individuals, nations, or warring fractions, they simply did not care. The only issue that concerned them was whether is was cost efficient. They were to her the worse type of criminals.

Crouched on one knee, Silvia peered around the corner. If she could only get to the alley, she thought, digging into her purse. Now she was being hunted like an animal. Silvia did not expect mercy, after it was all said and done, her employers and the international finance community would find out she had stolen billions out of spite. They'd have to kill her, just for the principle of it. How had her activities for The Organization been discovered? She wondered. Furiously, she found her plastic knife and ripped it from her purse. What few people knew except for Sister Clarice was that Silvia was a dangerous, crazy bitch. She felt trapped and the long-held savage beast rose to claim its time.

Rounding a corner, she ran into Spence, head of security for their building. Spence, always the gentlemen, stopped in front of Silvia and said, "Mrs. Williams, I've been in-structed to take you into custody. You most assuredly don't know it, but we've been looking for you since seven-thirty this morning. This way, please." He gestured, bowing slightly at the waist.

In the scant second it took for Spence to turn his head in the direction that he wanted Silvia to go, she had lifted knife and plunged it to the hilt into good ol' Spence's right eye. Blood spurted everywhere. A goodly portion splashed on her suit.

What hindered agents from apprehending Silvia this particular morning, was her tenacious drive for perfec-tion. She was not satisfied with her eyeliner, so she used the back entrance to her office instead of the front door in

order not be seen. There were a few things that she had
wanted to do with her makeup. The Federal agents had
walked in and did not see her standing in the dimly lit
bathroom. They had walked out and posted men at the
outer doors. Silvia slipped through the back. By this time,
her so-sharp secretary had informed them that there was
a rear entrance to her office. Now, she was loose in the
complex building. All the entrances were monitored by
guards and cameras except one — the one the mainte-
nance man with the security key uses. Efficient at everything that she undertook, Silvia had secured a key and
the code just for emergencies like this. Her mind raced in
unison with her feet. She had arranged the data in their
computer banks so only someone that knew about her
covert operations could decipher the codes.

Silvia was a top level operative for The Organization.
Not only did she launder money for The Organization, but
she cleaned money for the legitimate and illegitimate
enterprises in the city at large. Among her list of clients
was Striker. She had an automated emergency beeper
supplied to her by The Organization. When activated, it
sent a signal to Operations that something went wrong
and she needed to be picked up. It was activated the
moment she spotted the agents in her office. Her life was
at stake but much more was at risk. In her purse, she
held all the numbers for the banking accounts of The
Organization in thirty different countries on computer
disk. At all costs, these must be gotten to the right person,
specifically Miss Clarice. As Spence had fallen to the floor,
she had ripped his automatic from his holster. It was a
big, awkward 45. Silvia didn't mind. She gripped it
tightly. Hearing running feet, she ducked behind a water
cooler. A blur of boots passed within inches of her, then
receded down the hall. Inching along the wall, she gained

access to the remaining rear staircase that led to the alley.

She sensed a movement just above her. A hand holding a gun, appeared.

"Halt!" a voice shouted.

She whirled and fired. Three rapid shots, just like at the shooting range. The man fell from the upper staircase. Silvia gained the access door, dialed in the codes, then dashed into the alley where she found a beat-up Chevy Impala. She bent low to look inside.

"Got any gummy bears?" she asked.

"Yeah, but they at my grandma's house," a burly man with dredlocks replied. She jumped in and the automobile sped away.

That night, when the city had quieted, Miss Clarice sat in her regal, ruthless grandeur. Wearing a black silk granny dress, with fourteen caret gold buttons down the front, and sporting a brand new pair of highly polished granny boots, Mrs. C. received Lion and Silvia.

Silvia sat off to Mrs. C.'s right, quite at ease, lounging in an easy chair and holding a glass of golden amber liquor. She had changed into a black stretch suit. Lion, surrounded by two extremely large men, sat pensive in a straight backed chair facing them.

"Well, my beautiful lion cub, we meet." Sister Clarice paused, her eyes shone. "Just listen to what I have to tell you," she began, leaning forward as was her habit. "We are The Organization. We have many operations at hand and we also have a solution to your particular problem."

"I can handle my own problems," he retorted.

"Shut up, Lion Cub," she shouted, rising from her chair. "You have no purpose except to live and procreate — like a common animal. With us, you will have a purpose, and we have much use for a young man like yourself. We can offer you protection and safe passage. You'll be in a community of lions, Lion Cub. Just maybe you'll live the next couple of years. You know by now that long life is not promised to the foolish nor to the wise. Your individual struggle is fruitless. It will only end with your death. Like thousands of our young men, you'll be buried without reaching your potential. If you're intent on dying, die for your people. Make your death a lasting, meaningful one instead of another wasted life. Join us, Lion. We will be your mother, your father, your family of men and woman. This alienated way of living is a death unto itself, is it not?"

Lion was taken aback at the intensity and power of the old woman. He said nothing. Lion waited. What choice did he really have?

"If I do join you. What would you have me do?" Lion asked.

Miss Clarice smiled one of those rare smiles of hers, revealing slightly crooked teeth. "If you do decide to join us, you will receive three days of intensive ideological training. Then you, Lion, will be responsible to see to it that Silvia gets this briefcase to a certain government official."

"Where will this be delivered?" he asked, his curiosity aroused.

"Do you accept your responsibility, young Lion?"

"Yes, I accept," he quickly answered. "But there is one thing that I want."

"What is that, Lion?"

"Revenge for the murder of my gang family, and for the death of my cousin, Jamal."

"That you shall have, for it fits into our needs at this time. Sister Clarice never breaks her promises, especially concerning death," she added.

Sister Clarice sank slowly into her chair. A film of perspiration on her forehead reflected the light. She turned and winked at Silvia who had observed the meeting without a flicker of emotion. Silvia nodded her head in approval.

"You ever dreamed of going to Africa?" she asked.

"No, not really," Lion answered.

"Well, you're to see that she gets to Ghana, West Africa."

"I'm free to go until then?" he asked, looking as innocent as a lion possibly could.

"Of course not. Do you think we're fools? Lock him up. Your orientation and classes begin tomorrow!" she shouted. Lion was promptly shoved out of the room. She turned to Silvia, "If he demonstrates any sign of jumping ship or betrayal, kill him."

"That was something that you did not have to tell me, Sister Clarice," Silvia replied.

Lieutenant Flippo could be accused of many character flaws. One which he could not be accused of is not having nerve. He went to the meeting and steeled himself for what he knew must come. Maybe he could make a deal. Join a witness hideaway program and still have access to his money in that Swiss bank account. Striker would surely want him killed. Better him then me. Flippo resolved in his mind before attending the meeting.

Upon entering the room, Agent Brown instructed him to sit at one end of the long conference table. Brown faced him at the other end and his captain and used-to-be friend sat to his left. The other agents filed into the room as if they were going to perform an execution. Flippo had a hole card. He simply knew too much, not only about the known criminals in the city, but he knew the type of financial arrangements they had made with the area banks and politicians. If he couldn't fly, he'd take the city down with him.

The meeting was over and Flippo had never seen Captain Shultz so angry. He had made the deal. It was better then early retirement. The feds did not give a damn about the illegal drug money or his involvement with racketeering or murder. The agreement was this, that Flippo would help them to find out about this 'Organization.' He would also turn Striker over to them if need be. Those were Agent Brown's exact words. As to the political bigwigs, they would go on as usual. Shultz expected a city-wide crackdown. He was not only disappointed but dismayed at the attitude of the Federal agents.

Flippo had lied and hinted that he might have some leads on this so called Organization. Unbeknownst to the agents, Flippo did not have a clue as to the whereabouts of any organization other than the ones that gave him money each week. Little did Flippo know that his secretary had been on Striker's payroll long before he. The truth of the matter is that Flippo's secretary was instrumental in helping Striker get to Flippo. Striker was informed of the agents' visit and began to frantically make alternative plans. Number one priority — to eliminate Flippo.

As for Captain Shultz, well, it just wasn't his day. He was told that Silvia, after being discovered, had escaped, killing one guard and a federal agent in the process. She had fled into folds of the city.

Spring was just around the corner and the city was in for a long, interesting hot summer.

Tiffenie held Jason by the shoulders and positioned him directly in front in her. She straightened his tie and brushed at an imaginary hair on his jacket.

"Is this necessary, Tiffenie?" Jason asked, annoyed.

"You promised, Jason. I have to go to at least two of these office parties a year. It's expected of all senior staff. You know office politics. We'll make our grand entrance, grab a drink, stand around and look presidential. I'll make my rounds, then after a couple of hours of mindless chitter chatter, we'll leave," she stated, kissing him fully on the lips and grinding her hips into him.

"Stop, Tiffenie," Jason said, returning her wet kiss.

"Then, when we come home, I'm going to juice you," she responded.

"Juice me," he responded, a look of wonderment on his face.

On the way out of the door, Jason smacked her on her wide, full hips. Tiffenie giggled and said, "You ain't doing nothing but turning me on."

"Girl, you killing me," he stated, shaking his head.

The office party was held in one of the most expensive hotels in the city. Nothing was spared; prime ribs, shrimp cocktail and any type of alcohol that you could ever imagine was available. Tiffenie entered holding onto Jason's arm and greeted her work mates with her dazzling smile.

"Oh Jason, this is Mr. Rosenthal, my boss." She introduced the two. Rosenthal, resembling a stuffed pig in a black tux, seemed uncomfortable shaking Jason's hand.

"What type of business are you in, young man?" he asked.

"Securities," Jason replied.

"Now, that's a lucrative business. But it can go either way on you. Who's your broker?" Rosenthal asked, becoming inquisitive.

"Excuse me, I have to rescue Tiffenie. She gets bored so easily," said Jason over his shoulder to Rosenthal.

"How much longer," he whispered in Tiffenie's ear. She was leaning on a stool near the buffet table, bending everyone's ear. Three men and a women had surrounded her. It seemed like she was holding court.

"This is OK, Jason I'm getting to know more about the people that I work with. It is a smart strategic move, don't you think?" Her last phrase was one of his. She echoed it with a bit of sarcasm.

"OK, just enjoy yourself. I'll relax but, check on me now and then, OK?" he asked.

With a wave of her hand, Tiffenie was off talking about her work with her colleagues.

Jason scanned the room. There was Sandy, the woman that worked in Word Processing. Upon seeing Jason, Sandy sauntered over to where he sat.

"You undercover or something?" she whispered.

"Undercover? What are you talking about?" Jason asked.

"Well, this is an office party. I didn't know that security guards were invited." She walked in the opposite direction, her head in the air.

Jason, in disbelief, laughed out loud. People turned around and stared. Embarrassed, Jason pretended that he'd listened to a joke told by a group of people nearby.

Tiffenie came trouncing though, gorging herself. "I'll be ready in a few minutes," she said between mouthfuls of finger sandwiches.

"That woman who works in Word Processing, I think her name is Sandy..." Jason began.

Tiffenie, still chewing, stood her face inches from his. "Are you messing around with that trollop?"

"No, Tiffenie, I'm trying to warn you. She fronted on me in front of your co-workers."

Her eyes lit up, "Oh yeah?, What did she say?"

Jason explained to her. Tiffenie spotted her across the room watching them. She beckoned to her with her bent finger. Sandy looked to her left then to her right, then pointed at herself keeping eye contact with Tiffenie. Jason watched the unfolding event suspiciously. As Sandy walked toward them, Tiffenie walked out to meet her and gestured in the direction of the bathroom. Jason's eyes narrowed. They disappeared behind a free standing wall.

"Look, girlfriend," Tiffenie began, one hand on her hip, the other holding up the wall where she had pinned Sandy. "I hear you fronted off on Jason?", her breath hot upon her ear.

"He shouldn't be here. This is for upper administrative personal, not *security guards*." Sandy curled her lips when she pronounced security guard.

The absurdity of the woman's perception amused Tiffenie. "Don't you work in Word Processing?"

"Yeah, but I got a promotion to Administrative Assistant day before yesterday," Sandy replied defensively. Like a light bulb, it dawned on Tiffenie. This bitch was attracted to Jason and was trying to front off on him because he was not with her.

"Look, word processing bitch, don't mess with my man in no way or form or I'll stomp you," Tiffenie hissed. She flounced her bangs into place and strolled out to Jason.

Rosenthal had tracked Jason down, eager to gain more information concerning securities. "I realize that these things are confidential. However, I'm a reputable business man and I know of people in places that could triple your money," Rosenthal stated, his eyebrows arched.

Tiffenie grasped Jason's arm. "Well dear, let's call it a day. It was so nice, Mr. Rosenthal, we'll be sure to come to the next roast. The food, decor and the event were fabulous," Tiffenie said, flashing a smile.

In the parking lot, Jason had to search for their car. "There it is," he called to Tiffenie, who was in the next row. Vans parked on either side of their car blocked the view from the side. Jason unlocked the passenger side door and opened it for her. Tiffenie, instead of getting in the car, grabbed Jason and planted a wet sloppy kiss on his lips. She ground her hips into him. He grabbed her buttocks and stuck his tongue deep into her mouth. Jason slid his hands under her dress and clutched the fat part of her ass. This was his favorite part of her body. Tiffenie stooped and eased his throbbing member out of his pants. Licking the head, she engulfed his member, while on one knee on the concrete floor. Jason pulled Tiffenie to her feet by her hair. Helping her out of her panties, he spun her around and bent her over the hood of his car and roughly entered her. Caution thrown to the wind, Jason, in a fit of passion braced himself to get the best leverage possible. Tiffenie grunted. Jason groaned. They erupted simultaneously into a heap on the hood of Jason's car.

"Tiffenie, enough is enough. What if someone saw us?" Jason said, still panting. They were still lying on top of Jason's car. He on top of her, face down.

"Jason?" Tiffenie asked.

"What Tiffenie?" he gasped.

"Is this grey wire supposed to be on your car?"

"What grey wire?"

"This grey wire." The wire that she was referring to ran from under the hood into the crack in the car door near the hinge.

"Baby, I want you to move when I move away from the car," Jason said, pulling her by the waist, as he backed away from the car. He disengaged himself from her. He then pulled up his pants, and assisted Tiffenie with what was left of her dress.

Tiffenie, her hair in shambles and her lipstick smeared, turned to Jason and said, "I take it that there's not supposed to be a grey wire on your car?"

"No Tiffenie, I'll have to call someone to check it out."

"People from The Organization?" she asked, straightening her dress.

"Yeah, people from The Organization," he answered.

He and Tiffenie hid in the upper levels of the garage until people from The Organization arrived. They wanted to avoid her colleagues and any nosy security guards patrolling the parking area. Thirty minutes later, a beat-up Chevy van cruised slowly through the parking garage. Jason greeted them by knocking on the van window. Four men piled out and surrounded Jason's car.

"Somebody was going to blow y'all to hell," Simmon stated, dangling a packet of what he called *plastic explosive* in front of them.

"Is that what you took out of my car?" Jason asked.

"Yeah, this is it. We're doing another check to make sure there's nothin' else."

"How did you disarm it?" Tiffenie asked.

"You see, this device sends a false signal to the detonator. If everything goes right, the detonator receives this false signal and detonates itself, not the explosives." Simmon explained.

The bomb had been disengaged by splicing the wire. A small device with a built in timer had been used. Raffiki had directed the crew. Simmon had placed the device on the wire and ducked for cover. After a moment there was a loud click. Then silence.

"You a lucky man. How did you spot that wire?"

"I didn't spot it. Tiffenie did." Jason explained.

"You know this ain't the work of common gangsters," Simmon, the explosives expert stated, wiping his hands on a rag.

"I figured as much," Jason answered.

Three of the men had piled back into the van. Simmon had summoned Jason to the rear of the van while Tiffenie waited safely in the car.

"I'm going to submit my report to my superiors first thing in the morning," he said to Jason.

"It seems as if the intelligence community has gotten into the mix," Jason stated.

"It was inevitable," Simmon surmised.

It was four in the morning when Jason and Tiffenie arrived at her apartment.

"Jason, you're going to have to tell me more," Tiffenie stated gently. They were lying in bed with all the lights out. "If I had not seduced you in the parking lot, we'd be part of the cement fixtures," Tiffenie added.

"Yeah, I was thinking about that," he finally responded.

"Jason."

"Yes, Tiffenie," he answered.

"This is not fun anymore."

"Yeah, I know, Tiffenie," he rolled over and pulled her to him. They fell fast asleep.

Federal Agent Brown slept well that night. They had finally, definitely identified and located a legitimate member of this Organization. Flippo was not as dumb as he seemed. Jason's face had turned up with the wrong people at the wrong time. He didn't mind blowing Jason up to get things rolling. By shear luck or incompetence, Jason was alive and well. Jason was chosen because he had been seen more than once talking to Mr. Miller. Killing Jason was a ploy to get Mr. Miller to play his hand. Little was known about Miller, only that he was well respected in the underground Black community. Miller's dossier recorded that he had done six years hard time for an armed robbery. That was it, and that was fifteen years ago.

Ten days ago, a break through. A street informant had gotten word to the intelligence community that information was for sale concerning The Organization. When asked for proof of accurate information, Mr. James Miller had been named as a chief ruling member in this renegade Organization. After cross checking, Miller's name and face began turning up much too frequently. He was seen with an older woman at the Black Congressional Banquet. James Miller was treated with the same respect as congressmen and financial figures alike. Still, the intelligence community could not put this Miller in any type of category. At about the same time that his name and face began to show up at the most unlikely places, the rumor about a Black Organization began to take shape.

The discovery by the international banking community concerning Silvia and her activities had triggered a chain reaction across international boundaries. Huge sums of money previously unconnected, now were traced directly to the city. What brought the entire attention of the International Surveillance Community (ISC) into the picture was that this Mr. Miller was scheduled to have a meeting with one of the richest men in Japan.

To top things off, this Organization seemed to be a ring leader in illegal international currency exchange. It was a large scale operation. Funds totalling millions of dollars was invested in a research center in West Africa. Medical supplies, and technology coming from the United States was being imported to West Africa. By whom? These were the questions Agent Brown's superiors wanted answered. They knew about the illegal activities of drug money being laundered. Hell, it helped the economy; cocaine was a capitalist's dream. The overhead was relatively low considering the profits that could be made. Almost no risk whatsoever for the banking class of participates. The profits were outrageous. What the men at the top wanted were the men and women who dared to run an operation of that magnitude right under their noses. Politically this Organization must be crushed. These orders were given directly to Agent Brown. Like any good soldier, he would do as he was told and would even enjoy it, if by chance, it became gory.

"Hello," he answered the telephone. It was almost noon and Brown, in high spirits, was pondering what to have for lunch. "What? You mean they spotted it? "You're not just telling me this because the thing did not go off? — OK, OK. Who was the officer in charge? Get him down here to me, pronto. Got it?" Brown hung up the phone. His appetite had disappeared. Brown's great hair day had turned bad. Later, he would find that his day could have been much worse.

Flippo kept separating the collar of his shirt from the layer of fat around his neck. He did this by using his index finger.

"Look a little nervous, Flippo," Low Down stated, as he slid into the seat opposite him.

"I'm not here to play, Low Down. Let's get to the business," Flippo said. His voice just above a whisper.

"OK, baby boy, then business it is. How did the city's finest lose that young punk and shoot a seventeen year old girl in the process?" Low Down asked in an even voice.

Flippo shrugged his shoulders and then answered, "We got short notice and we're still looking."

"Well, let's talk about this Miss Silvia, the same one that you did a security check for us on, and, in your exact words, 'She is as clean as the Board of Health.'" Low Down's voice became charged, "Business is business and you turning out to be one bad investment. This Silvia bitch got some of our money and turned the city's international records into jelly before she left. We know she has to be connected because she would have needed help to transfer that much money. And, oh yeah, Flippo, what's with the Feds and all these intelligence people questioning our connections? You haven't turned on us have you Flippo?" Low Down asked, leaning towards him.

"Are you crazy? What would I gain by turning you guys in? I'm just as deep in this as you, maybe even deeper," Flippo answered. Flippo took a deep breath. "What's our next move?" he asked.

Low Down sat back in his chair. Something was wrong and Flippo was giving all the wrong signs. Why didn't he tell them about the Feds unless they made a deal?

"Everything is fine, Flippo. Forget about Lion. We'll deal with him if he ever shows his face in this town again. For now, stay low and get some info on the agents that are going around asking about some kind of organization. You know that Silvia was laundering somebody's money along with ours. That's why the figures did not come out right."

Low Down took a long look at Flippo, then looked beyond him at two men who were sitting at the counter sipping coffee. He slowly nodded his head.

"Well, Flippo, it's time that I took off. But you know the old saying —Those who forget the past are bound to make the same mistakes."

Flippo watched the receding figure of Low Down shuffling that ridiculous walk down the street. He silently shook his head. He had been around Blacks all his life and still there were many things that he would never understand. Flippo glanced at his watch. He decided to go to a movie. Fuck work. After all, he'd been found out by the police. If he didn't get Low Down jailed or killed, he was certain that Low Down would have him killed. This idea concerning an organization masterminded by Blacks was interesting. Tomorrow, the word would be on the street that he wanted information. Something was going on in this city without his knowledge and that was something that could be dangerous for him.

The movie he choose was *The Lawman* with Kirk Douglas. One of his favorites. Low Down — now why would someone sport a name like that? Flippo asked himself.

Unfortunately for Flippo, the two men that Low Down had nodded to at the coffee shop attended the same movie and sat two rows behind him. Midway through the movie, one of them got up and fired two silenced rounds into the rear of Lt. Flippo's head. A sudden gush of air escaped from his slack mouth. So ended the career of Lt. Flippo.

Captain Shultz was heart broken and Agent Brown was relieved. It meant they were getting close to something and he would not have to clean up after a dirty cop.

Thelma shifted in her chair. She jotted down a question that she would ask later and glanced at Tiffenie. Tiffenie seemed to be interested in the lecture and was also taking notes.

"The development of the human species is based on their collective commitment and understanding of their level of organization. If we observe the most powerful people world wide, we find that the level of organization determines their control, not only over their own lives, but the lives of others. The struggle is and always will be over the control of land and the ability to exploit its resources." The speaker paused, then pulled out a map which covered a good portion of the blackboard.

He continued, "The reason a minority of people control this much land is because of their level of commitment and the ideology that they practice." The speaker, a squat muscular man, looked at the clock. "It's break time people. You have exactly one hour. See you then."

This was the first series of what The Organization called political education classes. This was the level one classes everyone, no matter what level of their interaction of The Organization, had to attend. Thelma and Tiffenie had first sat in the back of the class. As the weeks flew by and the class had advanced, they became more interested and had subsequently moved to the front row. Today, Bobby appeared at the front entrance and motioned for them to follow him.

The building was once an elementary school. Like many small schools located on the predominantly Black populated side of town, it had been abandoned for busing's

sake. The building had been bought by community um-
brella organizations. The real deal was that The Organization had paid cash for the building, and used it, not only
for its own purposes, but for some of their front organizations and other community based organizations that met
its criteria as 'progressive'. The basement area and the
east wing of the top floor was for the exclusive use of The
Organization.

Thelma and Tiffenie were being led to the basement by
Bobby. Thelma, always one to pick up moods, sensed a
tenseness as they rode the elevator to the basement
depths. Thelma casually leaned against Bobby in the
elevator. The gesture was not lost on Tiffenie. Bobby,
unperturbed, held the door of the elevator while they
exited. They waited, then followed him down a dimly lit
corridor that dead-ended into a large door that was
painted a bright red. Upon closer inspection, Thelma
noticed that it was solid metal. Bobby stopped, pulled out
a card, and inserted it in a slot. He then dialed two numbers into his beeper.

"Step back, away from the door so that we can see all of
you," a voice boomed. There was a small camera lens set
at the top of the frame. They crowded into a tight three-
some. The door swung outward. Thelma gasped, Tiffenie
was surprised. Behind that obtrusive red door, was a
large office complex. A large, thick glass panel separated
the room in half. On one side were forty to fifty computers, all manned by a Brother or a Sister. The atmosphere
was serious. People were putting boxes on shelves and
labeling them. Some of the equipment was in various
stages of disassembly. Everyone at the computers seemed
in a crazed tempo. Somebody was moving and in a hurry.
Bobby escorted them through a maze of office pods, and
freestanding walls to the rear. They entered what seemed

like a small classroom painted a soothing yellow. Sister Clarice entered though a door that was covered by a standing blackboard.

"Oh Sister Clarice," Thelma stammered. It was obvious that Sister Clarice was on a mission. Around her eyes were circles that indicated that she had gone without sleep.

"Go get the lion," she said, motioning to Bobby. Sister was dressed in a light blue linen material. The top portion gave the impression of a military cut with a long matching straight skirt. She wearily eased her body into a padded chair. Her silence and demeanor suggested that everyone take a seat and be quiet. That is what they did.

Tiffenie had been informed by Thelma about Miss Clarice and was openly curious about this mysterious figure that seemed to have some hold over her life.

"How have you been, Sister Clarice?" Tiffenie asked, her voice echoing in the room.

Sister gave her one of those rare smiles. "In normal times, child, I would be happy to say at peace. But these are not normal times. Nor do I think that this is a social state that we've ever enjoyed on these shores. Now if you want to say, how is the revolution? I would say, all is well," she ended her tirade and caught Tiffenie in her hypnotic gaze.

The spell was broken when a young man was thrust into the room by another man that must have played football, he was so huge.

"I'm gettin' tired of muthafuckas pushing me around," the young man roared. Bobby entered at that moment and said to the young man something so faintly no one else could hear. Lion immediately calmed down. Sister Clarice sat there enjoying herself immensely.

"Come sit beside me, Lion," she said, motioning with her hand. Briskly, he snatched a chair and slammed it down beside Sister Clarice and flung his athletic form in it. Bobby looked at Lion, than at Sister Clarice and shook his head.

"Lookin' like y'all might deserve each other," he stated sarcastically. Sister Clarice rolled her eyes in his direction. "Are you through with me Sister C.?" he asked.

"No. Bobby, I want you to stay."

Quiet settled upon the room. As was anticipated, Sister Clarice cleared her throat and began. "As you all know, the national security forces have narrowed down our location to this city. The international security network has all but shut down our international communications. I said, almost all. We still have an ace or two up our sleeve. We had not planned on being discovered as a complete organization for at least four to seven years. Our economic growth and some of our overseas programs brought unwarranted attention to us. We had developed contingency plans to get our youngest and brightest into strategic locations all over the world. Africa must be our base of operations from now on. However, some among us, high up, have betrayed us. We are not beat by any stretch of the imagination, but there are some things that will have to be put in place at all costs.

"And that's where all of you come in. We don't know of all the traitors, but we know enough to not take any chances where we don't have to. Everything that you see in this building is being sent somewhere else. All the programs of training, whether ideological or technical, will be duplicated all over the world, including the major cities in the United States. There is no way this organization can be destroyed. In order that we have access to our wealth, to continue our struggle through the long term, you must see to it that all of these records get to designated places."

Bobby's face, most of the time impassive, broke into a smile. Sister Clarice laughed. "Yes Bobby, it's perfect. They're nobodies. No one knows them. A young hood, a petit bourgeois CEO, a security guard, and a stripper — it's too good to be true. Who would expect them to hold the future of this struggle in their hands and their hands alone?"

There was a rapid knock on the door. A man stuck his head in and beckoned Bobby to the door. Thelma watched for Bobby's reaction. His bland features flew into a violent twist. Something she had not seen in him. Bobby quickly whispered in Sister Clarice's ear. She was not as coy.

"He's here now?" she shouted incredulously. Then bring both to me now."

Bobby began to usher Thelma and Tiffenie out of the room. "They will stay," said Sister Clarice sharply. "It's time they understand the price that one will pay when we are betrayed."

A man and a woman were brought into the class room with their hands bound painfully behind them by a thin wire. A large gash pumped blood from the man's forehead. The woman was crying quietly. She too, had been beaten. Four men stood around the two who had been positioned in the middle of the room on their knees. Sister Clarice grabbed the man by his chin and arched his neck to meet her eyes.

"You scoundrel," she spat. The woman raised her head and tried to say something. Sister Clarice slapped her so hard her head popped back. The sudden sharp sound in the small room caused Thelma to jump. "Do you fully understand what you have done? I want your contact's name and I want you to tell me exactly what information

you've given to the enemy. And I want that information
now!" she screamed.

The small brown woman that Thelma had meet before
seemed just another animal at that moment. Energy
blazed from her slight form. She knew now why Sister
Clarice was feared. Even by Bobby.

The man began babbling uncontrollably. "Break his
arm," Sister Clarice ordered the larger of the four men.

Without hesitation, he bent the man's arm to an impossible angle and it snapped. The man howled. It caused
Thelma to shiver.

"I'll tell you. I'll tell you everything, if you let me live,"
he pleaded, sweat mixing with blood and dropping to the
floor. The room reeked of blood and sweat.

"Oh, do you think that we're savages that we would kill
you right here and let you lie in your own blood?" Sister
Clarice asked, her voice penetrating every crevice of the
room. The woman began to sway back and forth on her
knees.

"Mercy, Sister Clarice, mercy," she whispered loudly.

Thelma wiped her forehead with the back of her hand.
She was drenched and drawn into the scenario with the
same intensity. Tiffenie seemed in a trance. Bobby stood
by the door, his arms folded. He was not sweating nor did
he seem overly concerned about the spectacle of life and
death going on before his eyes. Thelma and Bobby's eyes
meet briefly and held. Thelma steadied her self. She knew
if Sister Clarice had anything to do with it, these two
would be dead before the day had ended.

A young woman dressed like Miss Clarice but with a
younger flair to the fashion entered the room. Along with
her, she brought a tape recorder and a notebook and pad.
Her expression did not change when she entered the
room. Sister Clarice spoke to her quietly and the woman

knelt and began asking the man and woman questions and encouraging them to speak into the tiny mike.

The man that they called Lion sat at ease alongside Miss Clarice. He acted like he was watching the warm-ups before a basketball game. Sister Clarice motioned to Bobby. He immediately began ushering Thelma and Tiffenie out of the room.

Nobody spoke in the elevator. Bobby calmly walked them back to their class. "I shouldn't have to tell either of you not to discuss anything that you've seen or heard today with anyone." he stated, then turned and returned to the elevator. After class, Thelma and Tiffenie hurried out of the building.

Once on the sidewalk Tiffenie said, "What the fuck have we gotten ourselves into this time, girlfriend?"

"It's serious, Tiff. We can't goof off. It could mean a lot," Thelma stated reflectively.

"I mean, it's like we don't have a choice. I don't mind doing something for my people but this is the extreme end of the spectrum, don't you think, Thelma?"

Their steady pace had taken them some distance from the school premises. Thelma slowed. "I thought about it even before today, Tiff. Something has to be done about the state of Black people. At least The Organization has concrete plans that we see really work. Look at the Literacy Program. The program to nurture teen mothers. Nobody is addressing those issues at the grassroots level like The Organization, at least nobody that I know of. I didn't realize that there would be so much opposition to Black people really controlling their lives. That's the real motivator for me. I have a right to mold my world in my interest and in my image just like everybody else. For someone to deny me that right infuriates me. It's like somebody telling me that I can't dance." Thelma frowned and continued to keep pace with Tiffenie.

"What about my job? Shoot, I make good money. I know that eventually this thing is going to come to a head. I don't think that it's wise that we be around to see it," Tiffenie stated.

"That's what I been telling you all along, Tiff. We goin' to get our orders, select a day and disappear. Like moon dust."

"Moon dust," Tiffenie repeated, looking at Thelma out of the corner of her eye.

"Yeah, moon dust. You ever see any?"

"Well, no," Tiffenie slowly answered.

"Like us, girl, won't nobody know nothing 'bout us or moon dust."

"I think you're weird," Tiffenie stated, frowning at Thelma. "Moon dust." She picked some grass from a nearby lawn and threw it on Thelma. "Moon dust," she repeated, laughing as Thelma ran, knocking the grass from her hair and shoulders.

Later that night, Thelma danced. It was a throbbing Caribbean beat that caught her in its web. She couldn't tell you what dance she danced that night. Letting it all go, her body responded to the high, intense inside rhymes of the timbales. The applause was deafening. Men and women alike stood on chairs and shouted for one more dance. Thelma's feet remembered the hard packed dirt spot just out front of her grandmother's home. She danced up the dust of another time and another place. Jackie was standing off stage applauding as vigorously as the audience. Thelma took her last bow and dragged her body to the dressing room.

"I don't know what to say, Thelma. Never have I seen anyone turn it on like you did tonight. Never," Jackie said.

"You don't have to sound so serious," said Thelma, toweling off the streams of moisture that her body had collected during her performance.

"You don't realize how good you are. You're creating another standard. Did you know people from the Creative Dance Studio downtown are here to see you. There's people here from the Ballet Consortium from Boston. You gave 'em something that nobody's ever seen. An erotic dancer, you've set a standard," Jackie said. A knock on the door caused both woman to jump.

"It's Dewvel. Are you decent?"

Thelma's eyes narrowed. "Give me five minutes will you?"

"Yeah, sure." Annoyance was detected in his voice. Jackie picked up the vibes.

"Is there anything you want me to do?" she asked Thelma.

"Did anybody see you come in here?"

"I don't think so."

"I want you to hide in the shower stall. I don't want to be alone with Dewvel unless I have to."

"Come right in, Mr. Striker, and have a seat," Thelma greeted.

Striker was not smiling, but it was hard to say what Striker was thinking. She'd play it by ear.

"Your show was par excellent, Thelma. Of course, this is something that you already know, I'm sure." He looked carefully around the room. "Are we alone?"

"Ye-s-s-s-s, we are, Mr. Striker," Thelma responded, stretching the s's of yes.

"First, bitch, I'm Dewvel Striker and few people play me.
I'm usually in their heads before they begin to think.
Now, we know that this Bobby muthafucka is one of
Miller's crew. I'm not quite sure, but I think that his
people or Organization have caused a lot of us honest
crooks grief. Feds snooping around so tough, we can't
operate properly. Everybody got cold feet. Even those low
life politicians running for cover. Ready to flush us down
the toilet if there is a knock on the door. Yeah, it's real
fucked up."

He paused to jerk Thelma's chair toward him by grabbing the leg and yanking it violently. The sudden motion
snapped Thelma head back. Striker ploughed his hands
under her robe and roughly fondled her breasts. Thelma
tried to jerk away. He snatched her head and held it
inches from his face. He continued in the same monotone
voice, "Then my boys telling me that you hooked with
some guy that ain't even got a car. So we checks this guy
out right. Oh, nothing personal, just protecting my interest. Turns up, he one of Miller's boys and that crazy bitch,
Miss Clarice. Now, the heat down on everybody and my
main girl, bringing me in so much dough, thinking 'bout
doing something that I would not like." He released her.

Thelma pulled her chair out of arm distance and glared.
Rubbing her neck, her mind went through every bit of
information that Striker had just told her. "You hurt me
Striker, and I don't appreciate it," she stated still rubbing
her neck.

"Exotic dancing bitch, I'll kill you here in this dressing
room and call the police. They will conduct a thorough
investigation and figure that a vagrant did it. Test me,
smart bitch."

Striker stood and walked over to Thelma. For some
reason, Thelma should have been frightened but she was

not. Yes, she was conscious of his ability and willingness to hurt her, but not afraid. If she got out of this, she'd never be without her 380, never.

"Hurt you? Thelma, you playing a game? I'm fixin' to break your fuckin' neck if you don't come clean with me."

Striker suddenly backed off. His kind feeds off fear. Thelma was not complying with his immediate need — that she fear him. He scanned the room. "Are we alone?" he asked suddenly.

"Unfortunately for me."

Striker walked to the door, "Boone, get in here."

Phats, the stage manager entered just before Boone.

"Where's Jackie? She's up next." He spotted her heels lying on the floor, they went to her Daisy Duke outfit. "Thelma, if you see her, tell her that she has five minutes. If she doesn't show, we'll have to put somebody else on. By the way, I'm honored to have witnessed your. performance tonight." He spun on his heel and walked out. Boone's bulk shrunk the room into half it's original size when he entered.

"She's coming with us, Boone. See that she's downstairs in my car in fifteen minutes." Striker walked out into the hallway and up the stairs.

Thelma turned to Boone. "You going to have to get out until I get dressed."

"You ain't leaving my sight, Thelma."

"Look Boone, there is only one way in and out of this dressing room. You ain't my boyfriend and you will have to leave until I get dressed.

Slowly, Boone looked around the room. "I'll be right on the other side of the door," he said, closing the door softly behind him.

"Jackie. Jackie, they're gone. Come out," Thelma whispered.

Jackie eased out of the shower stall. "Thelma, what are you going to do?"

"How the hell do I know with that gorilla standing outside my door." Thelma snapped her fingers, "You're on next, right?"

"Yeah, if I get out of here on time. I only have a couple minutes before Phats gets somebody else to go on stage in my place."

Thelma pointed with her finger and whispered into Jackie's ear.

Two sharp knocks on the door. "I'm coming in. You got five minutes, Thelma," Boone's harsh voice lashed out.

Jackie nodded, put on one of Thelma's stage wigs, opened the door and ran out. Thelma's and Jackie's body types did not match, but if Boone was convinced that Thelma was the only person in the room, it might give her just enough time to escape. Thelma ran the opposite way, turning the corner of the door quickly. She ran right into Boone and bounced to the floor. A woman screamed. There was a dull thud at the end of the staircase. Dewvel walked under the light of the shadowed hallway. He was smiling

"I guess your friend will have to come with us. You know what I don't like, Thelma?" She watched his hand lash out and felt it explode on her check. Thelma bounced against the wall and lay on the floor. "What I don't like about you, Thelma, is that you think you slick." He stood over her smiling.

The ride over to Dewvel's complex was silent. Jackie sat in the rear of the limousine with Boone and Striker. There were two other men up front. Thelma had never seen them before tonight.

"You OK, Jackie?"

Jackie was sitting opposite Striker, watching him with her gigantic eyes. She turned slightly and looked directly at Thelma.

"I hurt my shoulder on the steps." She turned back to Striker, "You didn't have to knock me down the stairs. Don't you have a mother or sisters? What kind of person are you anyway?"

Striker laughed then pinched her exposed thigh, twisting the flesh cruelly. Jackie shrieked and raised her hand to hit Striker. He smiled and she dropped her hand and moved over to sit next to Thelma.

Thelma pushed out her stomach muscles to feel the cold steel of her 380 against her waistband. It had been in her overnight bag, but she got it just before she ran out of the room. I guess exotic dancers were not supposed to be armed. Boone had not taken the time to search her, or thought her not worth searching.

The ride lasted forty minutes or so. They must be on the outskirts of town. Finally, the heavy automobile slowed to almost a halt. The front of the car nosed into a deep turn. The sound of gravel being crushed reached her ears.

It was still dark and it was the kind of night that you can see every star in the sky. Thelma stretched her neck and tried to get a good look around while they were being escorted out of the car and into a large white-framed house. As a little girl, looking at the stars, lying on her back in the grass, she felt that she could pluck one out of the sky like she did the lightning bugs. The stars screamed out to her tonight. She wondered if it would be the last time that she saw the stars.

Morrine answered the door. Her eyes were the size of quarters and her lips were parched, she had on a man's dress shirt and nothing else.

Striker mugged her in the face, pushing her aside. "Giken bitch. Been on that shit going on two days. Bet she just like those monkeys that base themselves to death." He shoved Thelma and Jackie into a sunken room that was hexagonal in shape. Turning to Boone, he said, "Take care of that business in the city and come back in about four hours. Bring two doggy bags back with you." He looked at Morrine. "Better make that three," he said, slamming the door behind him.

Striker entered the room and locked the door behind him. Thelma had pulled aside the curtains to find that the room just gave the appearance of being surrounded by patio doors. The curtains hid white-washed brick walls — there were no windows in the room. There was only one way in or out. She watched him slip the key in his trouser pocket.

"OK, Ms. Slick, let's see how well you dance," he said, slowly moving towards her. Morrine was sitting atop a black chair cleverly shaped like a cushion. He removed his jacket and shirt.

Jackie, sitting quietly on the couch, stood up and said, "I'll do anything that you want, Striker, just don't hurt me anymore."

Striker made a beeline toward her. Thelma waited. She could shoot Striker and take the key and maybe they would get away. Still, she was not sure. Striker was anything but a fool and he was awfully confident that the three of them could not overtake him. Muscles rippled under his satin black skin. Upon closer inspection, there were hundreds of tiny scars all over the upper torso of his body. Striker a victim, of course, Thelma reasoned. Sickness breeds sickness, and Mr. Dewvel Striker was a product. Pushing Jackie to the center of the floor, he savagely undressed her, ripping her last upper garment away with a fiendish expression stamped across his face. Thelma walked quickly towards him, pulling her weapon and cocking the mechanism. He turned to look into the barrel of a small caliber automatic.

"Don't even wonder if I'll blow your brains out, Striker," Thelma stated evenly.

"Well, why don't you?" he asked, turning around to face her.

"Turn back around, Striker, and get on your knees. If I have to repeat myself even once, I'm going to pump three rounds off into your sick, disgusting head."

Striker turned back around, then bent to his knees.

"Lock your hands together and put them on your head. You know the way, muthafucka," Thelma commanded, pointing the gun directly at the back of his head. Jackie and Morrine were in a state of shock. It took Thelma's voice to get them moving.

"Jackie, look in his pants pocket and get the key."

Jackie snapped to and got the key. Walking past Striker on his knees she kicked him as hard as she could.

"Ouch, I hurt my foot, kicking that shit," she exclaimed, holding her foot.

Thelma then remembered Morrine — too late. She came up behind her and jumped on her back. They were on the floor scuffling for the gun. It went off — two quick rounds. Morrine, in her crazed state, was as strong as a tiger. Thelma expected Striker any second to beat her to the end of her life. Pivoting, she rolled under Morrine's next attack to gain a superior position. Thelma crouched and pointed the gun at her chest.

"I really don't mind, Morrine. Test me," Thelma said, panting. Morrine raised her hands and backed to the far corner of the room. Striker groaned. Thelma whirled

around, the gun held out in front of her. He was down.
One of the shots had hit him in the lower back.

"We got the key. You see how they are? Kill both of them
and let's get out of here," Jackie said, her voice trembling.
She had gotten dressed and was walking toward the door.
A loud, heavy knock.

"You all right, Mr. Striker?" a man's voice echoed.

Just as she had thought. One men that came with them
was in another section of the house. Thelma crouched
next to Striker's head and whispered to him. He crawled
to the door.

"Yeah, everything is all right. Testing one of my new
guns," he said, leaning on the door. They waited.

"OK, if you need anything, me and Frank upstairs."
Muffled footsteps receded back into the house.

"Striker, it's like this. I don't mind killing you. I'm sure
you deserve it. I'm just not a killer, not yet anyway. If I
leave here alive, you will live. If I die, so will you. Now, if
you want to live, because I certainly do, get me and Jackie
to a car, free and clear. We'll all live to see another day."

"Give me the key. If it's not turned a certain way, an
alarm will go off," Striker said. His voice was still strong
despite the loss of blood.

Jackie rolled her eyes and handed the key to Striker.
She kicked him again. His eyes widened with the blow
but he did not make a sound. If she didn't have to, she
would not kill Striker, though she was certain that he had
planned to rape and later kill her. Someone else would do
it and soon, of that she was certain. Unlocking the door,
he pushed it open. Thelma stuck the gun in his ear.

"If I think that someone is going to try anything, this
thing will go off in your ear, Striker," she warned, pushing him ahead of her.

Striker had difficulty getting up. Jackie and Morrine helped him to his feet. They stumbled out into a lighted hallway. The staircase led up to the foyer. The front door was unguarded. They crept up the stairs, first Jackie, Morrine, and Striker. Thelma, last, held the gun tight in his left ear. She wanted to be certain not to miss. Music bounded down towards them from somewhere upstairs. Once outside, Jackie breathed a sigh of relief. She looked behind her and took a good look at Morrine.

"Hold on a moment, Thelma," Jackie said, holding up her hand. "Morrine come here," Jackie beckoned.

When Morrine was directly in front of her, Jackie hauled off and sucker punched Morrine right on the temple. Morrine was out like a light.

"That bitch. Bet she won't do no stupid stuff now," Jackie stated, rubbing her fist. Striker, bleeding like a stuck pig, took them directly to the garage and gave them the key to a late model pickup truck. Pulling out of the driveway, Thelma had to stop Jackie from backing the truck over Striker. They had tied and gagged him. Despite the circumstances, she had laughed when Jackie had stuffed her panties into his mouth. Now he lay prone in the middle of the concrete garage floor.

"Let's hope the muthafucka bleeds to death," Jackie said, easing the truck into traffic. They were on the main highway headed into town.

"We is all going to hell," said Thelma, shaking her head.

Bobby walked with his head up and arms flowing at his sides. His sister used to call the way he walked cruising, because his gait was so smooth. He had some time to spare and had chosen the long way to 80th Street by walking around the park. On the side streets, just off Winkler Ave., the street walkers lounged and plied their trade.

"Hey smooth walkin', you want a date?" a woman's voice called out.

He stopped and turned in the direction of the voice. Unlike a lot of hookers, this girl was pretty and did not looked used up.

"Naw, I don't want a date. I'm just cruising through," he replied. She walked toward him from the shadows. High yellow with flawlessly smooth skin; he judged her to be about 22 years of age. She had on cutoff jeans, a tank top and those crazy, high-heeled gym shoes. Bobby usually ignored street walkers, but today, found himself staring into light brown eyes.

"Well, what is it going to be? I don't have time to stand around and stare," she stated.

"What's your name? Bobby asked.

"Michelle. What's yours?

"My name is Bobby."

"Oh, so proper. Well, what is it going to be, straight sex or a blow job?" she demanded.

"I just want you to know that the people who care about you don't like you being out here," he found himself saying.

Those light brown eyes lit up. "You muthafuckin' men get on my last nerve. You think I want to be out here? All the shit that I've gone through and go through, and you out here being Mr. Judgement. If there were men I would not be out here anyway. So go fuck yourself," Michelle replied, her tone angry.

Hand on her hip, she flipped her hand in his face, turned and walked back into the shadow. Bobby could not help but notice the fat part of her hips jutting out from beneath those cutoff jeans.

He turned and continued cruising down the street. Bobby slowed as his thoughts turned to his sister. In their youth, times were better. He still remembered his father laying down the rules every Saturday morning over breakfast. He'd sit at the head of the table and lecture about having a strong work ethic and being a go-getter instead of being got by the system. Morrine would be sitting beside him and nudging Bobby in the ribs every time their father repeated one of his timeworn phrases.

Their mother, in response to their horseplay, would say, "Listen to your father, he only wants what is best for you." She'd say this while placing steaming plates of waffles and eggs in front of them. Then their mother would sit at the other end of the table and say the blessing.

Their world of caring, responsible parents and a comfortable home ended when his parents had gone out of town one Friday, and left Morrine and him at their uncle's house. He still could recall the telephone ringing early Sunday morning. Aunt Pearl's shrill scream woke him. When he and his sister were told that both their parents had been killed in an automobile accident, it felt as if the world had plunged into an abyss.

Naturally, he had assumed that his Aunt Pearl and Uncle Arthur would keep them. As soon as they got their portion of the insurance money as a result of his parents' deaths, they immediately turned Bobby and Morrine over to the Agency of Child Protection Services. After they were introduced to their new foster parents, Bobby had escaped through an upstairs window and caught a bus over to his uncle's and aunt's home.

He remembered standing on the front stoop for an hour ringing the door bell. Uncle Arthur kept peeking out of the window to see if he was still there. Realizing that neither his uncle or aunt were going to answer the door, Bobby, confused and hurt, walked across town to his foster parents' home.

It wasn't until he had gotten out of jail years later that Morrine told him of the sexual abuse that she had been subjected to from their foster father and brother. After the abuse began, she had begun a pattern of running away. One day she never returned. Morrine became a child of the street.

It was in prison that he had met Mr. Miller, the founder and architect of The Organization. Bobby had been recruited while locked down and received much of his political education from Mr. Miller himself. As soon as he was released, he began organizing. That was almost ten years ago. Still the knowledge that his sister was on the streets performing sexual favors for anybody that had fifty dollars, caused him a considerable amount of emotional pain. Helplessness fermented a different type of anger. He knew that his work on the streets would improve conditions so that other young men and women would not have to live that type of life-style, but that still did not ease his pain concerning his sister. Today was significant; a rare meeting had been scheduled between himself, Mr. Miller and Sister Clarice. Bobby glanced at his watch, he didn't have much time. His pace quickened.

"Hello Bobby," Miss Clarice greeted, hugging him to her and kissing him loudly on the check. Mr. Miller, always stoic, shook his hand warmly.

Bobby glanced around the apartment; this was the first time that he had been here. From the look of the file cabinets and fax machine, this was one of the Organization's secret communication centers. Miss Clarice brought him a cup of tea and seated herself in front of him along with Mr. Miller.

"I know that you're wondering why we've called this meeting, but be patient, listen and all your questions will be answered," Miller stated. He adjusted his straight back chair, the legs making a grating sound on the wood floor.

"Bobby, you've been in this Organization for almost ten years. Yet there are many functions of this Organization that you're not aware off. This was deliberate, but now we must reveal the history of The Organization so that, if anything happens to either Miss Clarice or myself, you can continue to carry the torch." Miller again shifted the chair along the wood floor then continued, "During the 60's and late 70's, an international counterintelligence organization began locking up, murdering, or delegitimitizing most of the active, progressive Brothers and Sisters worldwide. As you know, they broke the backs of the Panthers, Ram, All African Peoples Socialist Party, and the serious Black nationalist organizations worldwide. Even to this day, there are thousands of Brothers and Sisters wasting away in prison, not only in this country, but in the continent of Africa and in the Caribbean, due to their political activities and ideas.

"When I got locked down, I celled with a Brother who was a Panther. Of course, we formed study cells throughout the prison system and continued to learn. The main focus of our studies was to develop an organization that

could survive an international purge like the one that was
carried out during those turbulent political times. We
knew that it would have to be an international organization and that it would have to be revealed.

"As you know through your political studies, it's the
masses that make history. In order to combat a world
order that literally lives off the oppression of African
peoples, the masses of Black people would have to be
organized to the highest level possible. So, with the aid of
a few guards, lawyers, prison inmates, we began the task
of organizing our resources and people to, first, develop
individuals, then combat the forces that would hinder our
ability to seize real power. Now we are at the crossroads.
We've built the infrastructure, now it's time for you young
people, our second wave, to take the struggle to the next
level. The reason that we're telling all of this to you is
because you, Bobby, have been selected to 'pass the torch'.
So to speak."

Miller rose, and from behind the file cabinet, removed a
worn and battered leather carrying case and handed it to
Bobby.

"In that leather case are all the documents that cement
this organization together. All the contacts and study cells
in Cuba, Africa, the Caribbean, Europe and India. Guard
that case and information with your life, Bobby. And
remember, it is you who have been selected to carry the
torch."

Miller surprised Bobby once more that day; he hugged
him as he would have hugged his deceased father.

On the street, Bobby walked quickly to the bus stop and
boarded. He got off on the east side of town. After stash-
ing the briefcase in a burnt-out warehouse, he went home.

"So I'm to pass the torch," he said aloud to the dark room. Sleep didn't come easy, but eventually.

Sister Clarice sat alone in her office. Wistfully, she glanced around the room. It was in this very room that her life had taken on a meaning. The Organization had grown out of this very room. Plans had been made, time tables set, meetings held; dreams had methodically come into reality. Now, actual programs had grown from ideas. It was up to the young people. Would they be strong enough to carry on? No matter what? Mentally, she went through every phase of the political education classes that they had so painstakingly developed. Yes, it was sound. The seeds they had planted should grow into straight and tall trees — regardless of the conditions.

The time was near. She would meet with her shining stars this very evening. It might be the last time she'd see them. Age forced her to rise slowly. On the top shelf of her file cabinet was the lifeline of The Organization. A computer disk that contained the access numbers to The Organization's cash. It would be out of her hands after tonight.

There was one solid knock on her door. Only one person knocked like that. "Come on in, Miller," she said, her back to him.

"Are you prepared, Sister Clarice?"

"Certainly. We have had a long time to prepare. Don't you agree, Brother Miller?"

Miller started to say something but apparently changed his mind. He held Sister Clarice's arms from behind. She leaned back into him. The embrace was brief. He and this woman had seen the world spinning on its axis. Miller's blueprint for social justice could not have been realized if not for her. Miss Clarice's loyalty and intelligence was unequalled. Their bond for life was to right the terrible wrong that history had wrought on a people. Yes, she and about fifteen others of their cloak had cracked a dent in those mean city streets. They stood, but for a moment, feeling the mutual warmth. Briskly, they separated, a little embarrassed at their outward display of affection.

"Most of them are gone now. All our children, our work thrown to the far winds," she said, her features relaxing.

"Is your safe-house in order?" he asked, knowing the answer.

In creating The Organization, members were worried that a single purge could wipe out the hard core membership. To avoid that from happening, all major members were assigned the job to develop a safe-house they could go to for an indefinite length of time. This was for emergency situations. No one knew of the safe house, except the person that would be using it and the person or persons that lived at the designated house. It was someplace that nobody would ever associate you with. Provisions and funds were already stored there. Lines of communication were already installed. A special code was developed just for a time like this. The code was not written down; it was in each member's memory. Improper use of the code would certainly mean your life. It was Mr. Miller who had developed the system. He and Miss Clarice were to go into hiding this very day.

Their precautions were not unwarranted. They had been betrayed. Their informants downtown had warned them of the impending raid that was to befall their community center. As they spoke, rows of police vehicles were lined up at the station. Helicopters from the local National

Guard drummed incessantly like huge bumblebees overhead. Armored personnel carriers led the procession of
assorted military vehicles to cut off the freeway access
routes. The rest of the military array went to surround
the school-turned-community-center.

The power station was guarded. The Black owned and
operated radio station was commandeered. Agent Brown,
decked out in army fatigues and bulletproof vest was
apprehensive about the raid on the cultural center. Politically, it could be disastrous. The so-called Organization
had wove itself into the very fabric of the inner city. After
learning that the huge amounts of money had circulated
from this city, detailed traces were conducted. It was
discovered that The Organization had run its loan operations through the Black churches. It had set up and suc-
cessfully undermined the economics of poverty. It was felt
by some that, in a capitalist system, poverty to some
means wealth and riches to others. The Organization had
subverted the exploitative financial relationship the
banks of the city originally had with the Black-dominated
inner city. It replaced the banking system with one of
their own in which very few, if any, taxes were paid.
Under its tutelage, Black businesses had flourished. Dry
cleaners, fish markets, hardware stores, clothing outlets,
night clubs, etc., owned by Blacks, had all but run the
Korean, Arab, and Jewish businesses out of the inner city.
Agent Brown's orders were explicit. This Organization
must be annihilated at all costs. He had at his disposal
the economic and military might of the United States.
The status quo must be maintained.

Miss Clarice and Mr. Miller watched the army and
police vehicles take positions to surround the school. They
stood on a scaffold placed inside the tower for observation

of the school perimeter. The prearranged escape route was though a tunnel dug expressly for this purpose.

Clarice coolly ignored his first question about her safe house and said, "There are still so many records and documents that we couldn't move or destroy. How long do you think it will take them to truly know of our depth and width?"

"Only a couple of months. With their computers and information specialists it won't take them long. Some of the information that we left is incorrect. This was done purposely to slow them down and confuse them. In six months they should have enough to know of our complexity," he replied woefully.

Sister Clarice removed the computer disks from the drawer and placed them in a briefcase. They could hear doors and walls being smashed in by armored vehicles. The school was being raided on a large, military scale. Miller helped Sister Clarice down the narrow passageway to the tunnel. Before closing the door behind him, he set the booby trap. This tunnel would be used only once. Any other attempt to enter it would cause a terrific explosion.

"It won't matter," Sister Clarice began. "We've done what we were supposed to do. Now it's up to the young people."

"That's how it should be," Miller answered.

Later that night, in an old warehouse, long abandoned and desolate, Bobby watched for the signal from Mr. Miller. The ceremony for the inductions and promotions of the 'Long Robes' was about to begin. Miller, along with eleven other men and women, sat behind a long table on a raised platform. They were dressed in black silk robes. Below their platform were two tables with royal purple robs neatly stacked to a man's height. Bobby searched the crowd for Thelma. She, along with a hundred or more, were to be inducted tonight. This would be the last induction in this city for a long time — maybe for the last time.

The drummers began to beat out a slow, methodical walking rhythm. Two lines formed. The ceremony reminded Bobby of church and a fraternity pledge combined. The two lines walked and chanted in unison. 'We believe in our people. Accept our direction. Receive our love. In the cup of blood. Our sacrilege struggle. Forward ever, backward never.'

At end of the tables stood Sister Clarice and Mr. Miller. They helped the new inductees into their robes at the same time handing each a white envelope. This was followed by a brief ceremonial hug. The new inductee then proceeded to chant and form a line at the rear of the warehouse. Once this was completed, Mr. Miller rose to stand before the podium.

"Remember, it is man who is responsible for his own history. We define history as the continuum of past, present, and future events. As humans, we manufacture history everyday of our lives. As conscious humans, we accept the responsibility of history, materially and spiritually. The fate of our people has been dyed into the fabric of those robes. We accept the responsibility for our unwed mothers, of rampant prostitution by our youths, mothers, sons, sisters, and fathers behind this hated drug cocaine. We accept responsibility for our angry youth left to fight this psychological war alone, without the proper political education. Never in your life will you accept the oppression of your people in any form or manner. Real or threatened. We are alone in this struggle. We have no friends besides ourselves. For it is ourselves who will make our special brand of history. This history will eliminate negative processes and replace those with positive ones. You are officially sanctioned by those before you, as givers of life, of growth, and development. You have your orders. Do what you will. Bring our people victory whatever the cost. In that act, you will return our brand of dignity to our very doorstep and respect to ourselves and to the world."

There was no applause, only a heavy silence that was broken by the wild, upbeat tempo of Congolese drumming.

People began streaming out of the building. Thelma, agitated, began looking for Bobby. People weren't about to be standing around and gabbing. This was not like a regular graduation. The National Guard had positioned checkpoints along most of the main highways. While most of the people were hurrying out of the building, Thelma spotted Tiffenie fan dancing. Her butt rolling languidly beneath her purple robe to the beat of the drummers. Her eyes were closed. Thelma walked up behind her and smacked her on the rear.

"Ouch!" Tiffenie exclaimed.

"Girl, is you crazy? We got to get out of here. This ain't no party."

Tiffenie, unperturbed, said, "Yeah, yeah. Have you seen Jason?"

"No. I'm looking for Bobby. You know they're somewhere together."

At that moment Jason and Bobby walked quickly towards them. They hustled out of the building. Cars were pealing rubber onto the main highway. Tiffenie and Thelma took Jason's car and agreed to meet up with them later that night. The women had cleared all of their personal belongings out of their apartments and were ordered not to return to them. They were to meet up with Bobby and Jason later at a safe house.

"This car has a lot of pep," Jason stated, as Bobby gunned the engine of the late model Chevy.

"Yeah. We dropped a 350 engine in her and tightened down the shocks. It don't look like much but this baby can roll," Bobby replied.

Once in the city, they picked up Jomo and went to a section of town where there were abandoned and boarded up buildings. Jason led the way down some basement stairs. He shouldered a door open. Sifting around in the dark, he lit an oil lamp. It shed uneven shadows and shapes along the dank walls. The trunk that had been stocked and stored for emergencies was heavy. It took both Bobby and Jomo, sweating and straining, to drag it from under the floor boards. Jason fumbled with the key.

"Wow. Where did you get the artillery?" Jomo asked. His dredlocks rendered an intimate performance with the shadows on the wall.

The trunk lay open. Its contents were two Uzi pistol submachine guns, four nine millimeter automatics, a pistol grip shotgun, and fragment grenades. The weight came from the stacks of ammunition stacked carefully inside.

"Don't worry about where we got them. I just hope that you know how to get busy," Bobby said to Jomo.

"He knows," Jason affirmed.

"Yeah, I got my basic training with the Scorpios," Jomo answered, chuckling with glee. He was like a kid in a candy store.

"What's your choice, Jason? The shotgun or the Uzi," Bobby asked, while loading the weapons.

"Shotgun's fine with me. With these exploding shells, I'll be the one. Like Michael Jordan, last quarter of the game."

"Nigga trippin'," Jomo exclaimed.

"Is everybody ready?" Bobby asked, masking his voice so that he sounded like a television game show host.

Jomo squinted at Bobby. This was going to be some event, he thought as they climbed back into the Chevy.

"Shit, police and National Guard everywhere," said Jason.

"Why don't we postpone the hits on Striker and Low Down?" Jomo asked.

Bobby raised his right palm out toward Jason, who was about to reply, and said,

"After the raid on the community center, the general Black population had demanded an explanation. Instead of entering negotiations with the moderate Black political community, the police imposed a city-wide curfew. That incident where the only female African-American astronaut was dragged from her car by her fashionable Egyptian afro and thrown to the ground by a police officer, was the straw that broke the camel's back. Wholesale rioting broke out. Responding in kind, the city officials had ordered additional National Guard and Federal police help. Under cover of the crackdown, the relentless purge of the Organization's members are being conducted. Jason and Jomo, we have to kill Striker and Low Down and leave town to fulfil our assignments. Our original plans are no longer relevant."

"Whew, I guess we don't have a lot of choices do we?" Jomo said. He looked around the corner, "You ain't never lied about the police and National Guard," Jomo retorted.

On every corner, National Guardsmen stood, holding guns aloft, conducting searches at random.

"What's on the menu? Steak or Lamb," Jomo asked.

"We were supposed to get Striker first, but he has disappeared. We've looked everywhere. That really pisses me off because I got a couple of personal rounds to shoot off in

that mutha," Bobby stated, his voice charged with emotion. "No Striker," he continued. "We going to take care of
Low Down."

Bobby drove through a number of sidestreets and alleys,
avoiding the check points, where fatigued soldiers
checked for identification while thoroughly searching
vehicles.

"Now, you Brothers know that, if the cops stop us, it's a
shoot out. I ain't going to jail with all this shit in the car,"
Jomo stated.

"That's understood. They got a list. Me and Bobby are on
it. The police are looking for a lot of us that are associated
with the Organization. I don't know if they ID'd us
through surveillance or a snitch in our midst. But we will
shoot it out with anybody who tries to stop us," agreed
Jason.

Bobby slowed the automobile to a halt in back of a tall,
red brick building. It stood out in the block because the
shutters and gutters were painted black.

"He's on the sixth floor. I got a key. I'm going to sneak
up and let you in through the upstairs window just off the
fire escape. He keeps about three body guards with him.
Maybe more now since everything is out in the open. Keep
your spacing and kill anything that moves."

Low Down had decided that same day to move his operations to a more inconspicuous location. He had instructed
Dean to pull the Bronco around to the side. It would be
easier to load it from there.

Low Down was taking a large revolver from a desk
drawer when Scoot appeared at the door of the office. He
said, "We're almost ready, Low Down. I'm going to get
some artillery that we left in the basement and I'll meet
you at the side door."

Low Down nodded his head, still deep in thought. Since their scrape with Lion, it seemed like the whole world had gone wrong. Low Down had a nagging feeling about Lion. Twice they had missed him. He was not to be found anywhere. This Organization had brought down so much heat on the city. Their normally smooth operations were chaotic at best. That was no way to make money. Nothing was being moved except drugs. Low Down knew the score. To clean up their act, the boys downtown would sacrifice somebody like him to the public. The headlines would read, 'City's biggest dope dealer and criminal killed in shoot-out with police.' There would be a big investigation followed closely by the newspaper and local television stations. The entire incident would fade from memory after the first round of elections. Somebody would take his place and, gradually, things would get back to normal. He was not the one to take a bum rap. Low Down refused to be used by anyone. Striker was his go-between and major connection as far as money and opening markets. Mostly it was just business between the two. Striker was not his boss. Low Down did not tolerate a boss. If he went down, it would be by his own volition. He checked the ammunition in his revolver and snapped the bolt shut.

As soon as they got out of the car, Jomo held out his hand and said, "Naw, man this don't feel right. There's too much open ground between us and the building."

His words were cut short. Coming from around the building and getting into a Bronco, was Low Down and his crew.

Little Mack spotted the three armed men at the same time that Jomo spotted him. Little Mack raised his automatic pistol and ran off a thirty round clip. Bobby, Jason and Jomo dived to the ground for cover. Jason raised up from his prone position and unloaded three rounds from his shotgun, the exploding shells blowing fist sized holes in the parked Bronco. Dean, Turtles replacement, propped up his AK 47 on the hood of the Bronco and ran off a twenty round clip. A barrage of gunfire erupted from this barren spot in the city.

Bobby ran back to the car, dodging bullets. He U-turned and blew the horn, signalling Jason and Jomo to follow. Jason was pinned down in the middle of the lot beside the building. He had five clips left and, at this rate, in a minute or so he would be out of ammunition. Bullets continued to plow up the ground around him. Jomo had the advantage of a mailbox and was shooting from a crouched position. He was midway between Jason and Bobby. If he ran now, there was a good chance that he could make it to the car, but that would leave Jason stranded. That he wouldn't do. He put another clip in his Uzi and shouted to Jason.

"I'm going to give you some cover."

Before Jason could protest, Jomo sprinted towards the Bronco firing rapidly. Halfway, he stopped and retreated. His sudden attack allowed Jason to get to a standing position. They ran towards the car, turning and shooting at intervals. Jomo got into the back seat leaving the car door open. Jason jumped in head first. Before Jason had closed the door, Bobby floored the souped-up Chevy. Glass shattered and flew throughout the automobile as the car was sprayed with bursts from an automatic machine gun. The smell of burning rubber filled his nostrils. Jomo groaned.

"Jomo's hit!" said Jason, turning around in his seat. The rear seat was smeared with bright red blood.

"I'm not hit bad, just my shoulder," Jomo explained, grimacing.

"We got to get him some medical treatment, Bobby," said Jason.

"We got to get out of the city first," said Bobby.

Turning the next corner, they ran right into a roadblock. Some kids on bikes prevented him from making a U-turn in the middle of the street. A car with an old couple pulled up behind him.

"Y'all ready?" Bobby asked, tensely watching the guards coming towards them.

From the back seat there was the solid click of a round being chambered. Jason cradled the shotgun in his arms. He looked around. There was very little cover and a lot of police.

"Oh well," he said, not to anybody in particular. Jason waited until the guard stuck his head in the window. Then he whipped up his shotgun and blew the guard's face off. Jomo rose up from the seat and rattled off a clip.

Bobby backed up and rammed into the old couple's car to make room for the U-turn. The quickness of the assault proved to be to their advantage. Deftly, Bobby headed the car in the opposite direction, the rear end of the car trembling from the abrupt acceleration.

"We in the shit now," Jason said.

"Not if we ditch this car. And I mean right after the next corner," Bobby replied.

"Jomo. You ready? Jason asked, turning. "JOMO!" he shouted.

A bullet had splattered Jomo's forehead, leaving brains and blood plastered to the glass and seat. From the neck up he was unrecognizable. Jason heaved, it felt as if someone had kidney punched him.

"Jason, get ready!" Bobby shouted against the screeching of the engine.

Most of the windows had been blown out. Glass was everywhere.

"He's gone. We got to ditch this car and I mean right now!" he screamed. "Now!"

Both men opened their doors and rolled out onto the pavement, letting the car careen down the street. Large helicopters with sensors scooted back and forth over the sky overhead. Police and army vehicles of all types filled the area. The hunt lasted well into the night. Still the hunters were disappointed. Many a man was roused from his car or home that night. But not the two that had shot up one of the police checkpoints. It took two days and a night for Bobby and Jason to reach the rendezvous with Tiffenie and Thelma.

"Where in Heaven's name have y'all been!" Thelma screamed. Bobby had to keep knocking on the window to wake her. Tiffenie, stuffed in her junior sleeping bag, would not wake short of a natural catastrophe or Jason coming home.

"We had a shoot-out at a check point on the North Side. We ditched the car." He paused, his eyes grew wide. "Jason's not here?"

"No. I thought you two were together," Thelma replied.

"We were, but we split up at the river. The authorities were looking for two Black males our age. We figured that if we split up we'd have a better chance." His voice trailed off.

Both of them whirled around responding to the hard rapid knock at the door. Bobby walked to the door and yelled, "Who is it?", holding his gun aloft.

"Open the door. It's me, Jason."

Tiffenie came out of the room yawning. She had on an oversized baby panda pajama outfit complete with feet.

She enveloped Jason with a hug, wrapping her legs around his waist. Jason, exhausted, relented to the weight of passion and fell slowly to the floor with Tiffenie glued to him. His mouth was muffled, "Tiffenie you got to let me up. I got to bathe and get something to eat."

"OK, I'll fix something for you and Bobby. Y'all tell us what happened these last two days," said Tiffenie, relinquishing her hold on Jason. She began to prepare a meal for the two men.

"It's been on the radio and TV about that shoot-out at one of the check points. I didn't think that it concerned you two," Thelma stated." She openly hugged Bobby to her. "You're cut!" she exclaimed.

"That's from all the flying glass when they sprayed us," Bobby explained. Between mouthfuls of mashed potatoes, greens, and beef neck-bones, Bobby and Jason accounted for the last two days.

Jason, laying on the floor, said very little, his mood cloudy. The apartment in which they were staying consisted of one room. A small kitchen and a large bathroom. Fed and showered, Jason decided to break the news about Jomo's death to Tiffenie in the morning. He told Bobby to wait until tomorrow before he told Thelma.

"Why did you get a junior size sleeping bag, Tiffenie?" Jason asked. "You can barely fit in it." .

"I wanted to be stuffed like a Christmas stocking. It makes me feel secure," Tiffenie answered.

"Tiffenie, I truly believe that you are crazy. Well, we both can't get in that bag. We'll have to sleep in mine," said Jason.

Once they were snuggled in, Jason fell fast asleep. Tiffenie watched him, propped up on one elbow.

On the other side of the room, Bobby lay nude in a double sleeping bag. Thelma had purchased one but decided to slither into Bobby's, wearing only bikini panties and a white tee shirt. He ran his hands over her buttocks and squeezed the mound between her legs. A breath of air escaped her lips. Thelma nuzzled and licked his ear. She ran her hand over his muscled stomach and further down to encircle his penis, rubbing the top of it with her thumb. Bobby's senses ignited; he groaned aloud. She lay in his arms. He dipped his shoulder and positioned her on top of him. Thelma helped him pull her tee shirt over her head. He sucked tenderly on one breast then the other. Bobby took his time licking on her nipples. Jolts of passion caused Thelma to wail loudly. He grabbed her buttocks in a vice grip and positioned her pelvis over his mouth. His tongue slithered slowly into her depths. Incoherent sighs and moans escaped from her lips. Their bodies slick with sweat, Bobby lowered Thelma onto his stiff manhood. Her powerful thighs and hips rotated and churned vigorously. He shuddered, then Thelma, with a mighty heave, came to a mind-shattering orgasm. They lay panting, their bodies still joined.

"Oh Bobby, if you only knew how much you mean to me," Thelma whispered.

"I'm beginning to care for you too, Thelma," he responded. She staggered to the bathroom. When she returned, he was fast asleep.

Tiffenie, on the other side of the room, snickered, "You go, girl. Work that man."

"Shut up, Tiff. You will wake them up," Thelma replied smiling.

Tiffenie still propped up on her elbow said, "A freight train running though this very room could not wake them up." She paused and walked into the kitchen. "I think Jomo is dead," she said, lowering her voice.

"Yeah, I think so too. Bobby hasn't mentioned him. I think the body they got out of the car was Jomo's," Thelma said. She folded her arms, her features sharpened. "Tiff, If I tell you something, will you freak out?"

"We friends to the end, Thelma. You can tell me anything. I might freak out, mind you, but I'll always be in your corner," Tiffenie answered.

"This is the first time that me and Bobby have done anything. I want to be honest with him about me and my past." She paused and looked Tiffenie squarely in the eyes.

"I had an affair with my dancing instructor when I was seventeen years old. My dancing instructor was a woman." She paused to see what type of reaction she would get from Tiffenie. She continued, "I want to tell Bobby everything about me. But I don't want to sacrifice this relationship for anything."

"Have you had anything to do with any more woman after that?" Tiffenie asked.

"No. Just with her. She was the only one who ever showed me any tenderness. I had been placed in an orphanage when my grandmother died. When I realized what people thought of gays, it sent me through a serious emotional trip. That's the real reason I ran away from the orphanage. I wanted to break up with her and she threatened me. Until that time, I didn't think anything was wrong with it. After she came off like that, I got hat."

"Thelma, I think your instructor took advantage of you. Wait before you say anything to Bobby. I think that he can handle it, though," Tiff stated.

"How about you, Tiffenie. Can you handle it?" Thelma asked apprehensively. Tiffenie bear-hugged Thelma to her.

"We friends to the end," Tiffenie whispered. Their tears blended and fell onto the hardwood floor.

While most of the city slept, there were others that choose the night hours to pursue their trade. Agent Brown was one of those rare gems; he never slept soundly during assignments until the job was done. It was true that he had snared many of the members of The Organization, however, he did not get any of the leaders. They're still somewhere in the city, of that he was sure. He had to give them credit. The architect of this organization was a genius. They had brought untold damage to The Organization, but the way it was structured, you could never get a firm conceptual handle on it. Brown would personally like to nail this genius's head to a wall. After carefully going over the little information they had acquired about The Organization, the man named Miller was one suspected of being the creator and architect. He and this old women named Sister Clarice kept popping up. Well he'd find them if he had to conduct a neighborhood by neighborhood, door to door search. Fuck civil rights, this had to be crushed before the idea took hold.

He held his head between his hands. What if they had an organization in most of the major cities? It rang a deadly bell in the back of his head. Advanced planning, training, development, research, and implementation were evident. Russia could not be completely ruled out. It didn't make sense. The future of this world was tied to their relationship with Russia. They would not risk that for some unruly Blacks? Surely, they had not conceived and implemented something as advanced as this on their own? Castro. Perhaps this was something for him to do while he's in his death throes. Still they had found no external connections.

He picked up the phone. "Has the Advanced Inner City Tactical Squad gotten here?" He paused. "Send Commander Hunter to my office right away. By the way, have they found those guys who shot up the check point? — Tell the men to gear up, we're conducting sweeps tonight." Agent Brown hung up the phone and leaned back in his chair. Something was bothering him but he could not put his finger on it.

Sister Clarice at that moment was sipping her favorite wine and stroking the velvet cheek of Silvia. Lion was somewhere in the house listening to that Godforsaken rap music. This would be the last time she would see her lovelies. Her Silvia and her Lion.

"Yes dear, you must go this very night. Your assignment cannot be compromised. It means so much to so many people." Sister Clarice smiled. Silvia meowed under her caresses.

"I'll miss you terribly, Mama Clarice," Silvia said.

"And I you. But you have to understand that you are an extension of me. All the money and wealth that we've collected is for the future. You have to make that young lion in there understand it too. My love for you is a love given to us by our ancient elders. It's the kind of love that knows no sacrifice too great to accomplish our task. When you leave me, you will be gone from my sight, but never from my heart."

Silvia sat on the overstuffed stool. It matched the easy chair that was Miss Clarice's favorite. She clutched Sister Clarice around the knees.

"You're the only one that has loved me. You showed me the meaning of purpose. You and The Organization have given me so much. You know that I'll never let you down," said Silvia.

She rose and walked to the mantle piece over a long, unused fireplace. Taking a velvet covered jewel box from it, she turned and handed it to Sister Clarice. "This is for you. I stole it at a diamond display in Zurich." She chuckled. "They never, even for one minute, suspected me. Now, they know. I so enjoy doing naughty deeds. The naughtier the better. It makes me feel so-o-o-o good," she beamed, her white teeth flashing.

Rolling the glimmering gem in her hand, Clarice appraised its value. It was priceless. You wouldn't dare try to sell it. The diamond was too rare and valuable.

"This is remarkable, Silvia. But, what would I do with it?"

"Sometime, if you ever miss me, hold it up to the light. Look into it and you'll see me. Your Lovie, your Silvia, always, Mama Clarice."

Sister Clarice pursed her lips, then abruptly said, "Within the hour, I want you and that young lion gone."

Miss Clarice brushed Silvia's silky cheek again with the back of her hand. Silvia arched like a cat, then purred. Promptly, she went and beckoned Lion to pack.

Sister Clarice rolled the sparkling gem in her hand. From her upstairs window, she watched the figures of Silvia and Lion disappear into the deepening gloom of twilight. The shadows on the sidewalk eventually swallowed their forms. "May the winds of fortune go with you, my lovelies," she whispered, holding the gem against her cheek.

Just the other night a sense of foreboding had enveloped her. Now that Lion and Silvia had left, her mood had lightened. After all, her work was done. It was up to those such as Lion and Silvia now, the young people. It was their world. It was up to them to take it, whatever the cost.

Striker bent on one knee. His lips were close to the man tied to the chair. Striker was thickly bandaged, and moved awkwardly, bent waist. Shifting his weight, Striker took a deep breath. This torture and interrogation had been going on close to four days now. The combination of bright lights, cigarette burns to the man's mouth, face, and testicles had finally produced the desired results. The man named Kamau was a respected member of The Organization. He was stronger then most. People talk shit about being tough, but torture was real. In time, anybody would break, given the right incentive. Kamau writhed and thrashed. He was in his death throes. Lack of water and the abuse suffered had caused the man to go into shock. It did not matter. Striker had enough information to know where Miller and Miss Clarice were holed up.

He motioned for Boone. "Call Agent Brown and tell him we have some information that he might value."

In the wee hours of the night, a caravan of dark green military trucks penetrated the north side of the city. Like a monstrous black cloud, the caravan spread out to totally engulf that section of the city. Agent Brown was efficient. Droves of helicopters hovered and drummed overhead while thousands of troops debarked from the trucks and began the slow methodical neighborhood door-to-door search. It was not in the lower classes of homes or apartments that many of the leadership had chosen to stowaway in. The large houses that were well kept, with the taxes currently paid, were the homes of choice. It was doctor's and lawyer's, and in some cases, legitimate politician's homes that were commandeered by the Central Crew.

Sister Clarice resided at the home of a retired dentist. His wife had died and his children had families of their own. He had been recruited by Sister Clarice herself. When she appeared on his doorstep unannounced, he had showed her the quarters in which she would be living and, with a nod, retired to the lower half of the house.

It was about three-thirty in the morning when a distant noise caused Sister Clarice to open her eyes. She lay stretched out flat on her back in a queen-sized bed with a canopy. The clamor had a familiarity that drove tiny little daggers into the base of her consciousness, screaming for her to wake.

Shoot, I'm old. Sister Clarice thought, her mind and body slowly joining the physical world. Her eyes wide open, Sister Clarice listened carefully. Heavy trucks, men and metal. Were they here already? Chopper blades pounding the night air overhead, scanning. Either they were betrayed or somebody had been broken.

Well they had planned for it, hadn't they. The many children that were inducted recently had been one of their better crops. Except for her personal comfort, it really didn't matter. She lay completely still, listening. Heavy concentration of amour vehicles, trucks, and more men. Sister Clarice rose and began to dress. There was a number she could call. Maybe I should get lifted out of here. But for what? Her work was done.

That old rascal, Miller. Amazing — ahead of his time in planning and setup. He was a scoundrel, though. It was he who gave the vest to Sister Clarice. It was called 'the option vest.' She struggled to put it on before she donned her sweater. The snaps were positioned at awkward angles.

"Ah, now I'm ready," she said aloud. Sister Clarice breathed deeply. All was better now that she had options.

Peering out of the upstairs window, she used her stargazer. The infrared light gave shape and form to moving shadows. They were about four blocks away. In an hour or so they would be here. Maybe she should run for it. Again she asked herself. What for? She retrieved the diamond from its box and held it up to the light. Exploding luminous points of light dazzled in its depth.

When the soldiers came to her house, she let them in and introduced herself formally. She also informed them that she would like to speak to the commander of the operations.

Agent Brown was ready to pinch himself. Ecstatic with glee, he swooped down from a command helicopter, not believing his luck until he actually saw and talked to her himself. So they caught the old woman. Sister Clarice. Wonder if that was her real name? Brown bounded up the flight of stairs.

"Scan the woman for explosives," he stated before entering the room.

"She's been scanned sir. We cannot detect any electrical device on or in her. The woman was patted down, sir. We think she's clean."

"Does anybody else know that we've captured her?" Agent Brown asked the military inspector.

"No Sir. Nobody even knows who she is besides the intelligence boys, sir," the inspector answered, saluting stiffly.

Agent Brown entered the room with his hands behind his back. His manner stiff and formal. If this woman was who he thinks she is, she would never make it back to the

station. He must not show any of that liberal weakness.
She would be interrogated to maximum then, if still
living, shot. Those were not wishful emotions. Those were
orders.

"Well, well. I'm privileged to meet the nefarious Sister
Clarice.

Clarice sat tranquil in her favorite chair. She knew by
the way this was being handled, she was not going to be
arrested. She would be tortured, then shot. It was her
way after all. Mr. Miller called it playing hard ball.

"And who do I have the privilege of meeting?" she finally
responded.

"I'm Agent Brown. Agent in charge of operations to
crush this accursed Organization.

"Accursed," Sister Clarice repeated, seemingly confused.
Standing she walked around the room to stand in front of
Agent Brown. "I did not expect to be found this soon," her
voice trailed off.

"Without the help from a Mr. Striker, it would have
taken us considerably longer to find you. However, the
reality is that we now have you. Cooperate, things will go
in your favor," Brown answered.

They were both fishing for information. She, out of curiosity. He, out of need.

"We can make it easy for you, Sister Clarice. No harm
will come to you and nobody will even know that you
talked to us. I might even work out a deal for you. Let's
say, instead of jail, maybe a long trip to a Caribbean
island," Brown said, holding out his hands.

"So Mr. Striker helped you, did he?" She waited until the
room had filled itself with silence before she spoke, again
maneuvering. Clarice watched Agent Brown as intently
as he was watching her.

"I'd like to add that Mr. Striker told me, if I had any trouble with you, to call him."

Sister Clarice feigned terror and confusion. "You mean you would actually work with a monster like Dewvel?" she asked, her eyebrows arched.

"So, if you don't answer questions for me, we will contact Striker," he threatened.

The old woman clutched at her heart and slowly sat on the footstool. The same one that her Silvia sat on when they were last together in this room. She smiled, turning her head away from Brown.

"Who are the leadership members in this group?" Brown asked his eyes hard.

"You know that I can't tell you that," she answered her voice barely a whisper.

"I really hate to do this. You're an old woman and all. But it looks like you're uncooperative attitude has forced my hand. Striker is on his way."

Sister Clarice did all she could to conceal her delight. Brown was becoming wary. This old woman just was not acting right. She did not tell him that it wouldn't matter if she told him everything she knew. The seeds of the idea were scattered to the far winds. They would take hold or die, the success depending on no single individual. Even if only half of the money belonging to The Organization found its way to their operatives, all would go well. Brown would not tell her that Striker was the only person who could properly identify Sister Clarice. At least the only person that he knew. All the photos they had of her were inadequate for positive identification. Sister Clarice possessed more than 50 wigs. One of her many skills was as a makeup artist. This is how she had made her living a good part of her early life. Touring with a theatrical troupe. Brown wanted every step to be confirmed.

A chopper beat directly overhead. "I think that's your friend, Striker," Brown said, walking out of the door.

Clarice snapped her head away from him. Brown narrowed his eyes. He guessed that she was afraid of Striker and did not want to show it. Her eyes seemed to gleam at the mention of Striker's name.

"Don't let her out of your sight," Brown instructed the guards on duty.

Alone, Sister Clarice made herself comfortable. She smoothed the pleats of her skirt and made sure that the blue wire would snap onto the red wire when the time came.

Just three blocks up the street, Thelma and her company of three were making preparations to escape the military crackdown.

"I know of a place downtown were we can stay at least for a day or two," Jason said as he was loading a plastic bag full of toilet paper into an overstuffed duffel bag. "We'll have to get out of here before they shut the neighborhood down completely. There is a corridor down by the river. It was used way back when by farmers when they wanted to go to the city and sell their produce. It goes all the way to the other side of the river. Hopefully we'll get some type of diversion to cover our escape," Jason stated.

"Hello, Sister Clarice," greeted Striker. He walked with a pronounced limp, bent over a crooked walking stick.

"Did one of my children do that?" she asked mockingly, her voice innocent as a child.

"Yes, she did. You should have seen what I did to her friend. Jackie's the name, I believe. I tortured her and Morrine to death. What I did to one I did to the other, both watching. That's my thang, you know." He paused.

As was his nature, Striker was leery. "Has this room been checked?"

Brown said, "Thoroughly, and she's been searched for metal and plastics. Everything done by the book. That's why I'm in the position I'm in. You remember that, Striker," Brown replied, making a mental note that he must appear harsh and insensitive around these people.

"Let's get to it. You know the information I want. Whatever you do, don't kill her until you get the information that we need. After that I don't care. Our people will dispose of the body. This thing has to be handled in a certain way due to its political nature. I'm sure that you understand. Seeing that your very ass hinges on you getting the information from this old bag, it should not be too hard."

"Striker!" Sister Clarice shouted, demanding his immediate attention. "Do you remember my Lion?"

A puzzled expression was her answer.

"You'll not stay and join us?" Sister Clarice asked, standing and adjusting her belt.

Striker's eyes grew wide. That's the last thing he or anybody else in that building saw, for, at that moment, a tremendous explosion erupted from the inner folds of Sister Clarice. A blast so powerful that the top of the house fell squarely into the street, smashing into thousands of deadly fragments. Old fashioned dynamite could not be detected with the modern methods. Mr. Miller, that scoundrel, figured he'd let modern technology fool itself, at least this once. Unknowingly, Sister Clarice, in her final moment, gave four of her children the distraction they needed to reach the river and safely cross.

It turned out that the white envelopes were a double-edged sword. Each person that was given an envelope that night at the 'Induction of the Long Robes,' had an assignment to carry out. For Thelma, it was to deliver a computer disk to a certain person, at a specific time and location. The city she was assigned was Houston, Texas. Unfortunately, Bobby was to go to New Jersey and Jason to New York. She couldn't figure out why Tiff and Jason had the same city and she and Bobby were assigned separate ones.

"What's this about? I don't like this shit at all, Bobby." Thelma ranted, waving the opened envelope across his face.

"It don't mean that we can't hook up again, Thelma. It just means that we have to complete our assignments on the time schedule given. We can't all go to each city. The timing would not be right. So after you do what you have to do in Houston, either I'll join you there or you'll come here. Pure and simple," he admonished, arms open to encircle her.

She pushed him away and folded her arms, sticking out one leg in front of the other. Her lip and hip jutted out at the same angle. Bobby thought her beautiful she was when she was like that. Somehow it reminded him of antelope on the vast African plains. That look was unique to African women.

"Look Thelma," Bobby began again. "All you have to do is deliver your disk. Get on a bus and hook up with me in New York."

"I thought you were going to Jersey," she stated.

"Oh, You don't trust me now? Look Thelma, what I have to do in Jersey will be a one stroke thang. Then we're going to start building The Organization again in New York. We have all the floor plans. First we survey the area, select a neighborhood that meets certain criteria, and begin infusing the concept of our ideology into the lives and 'culture' of the people. House to house, block to block, neighborhood by neighborhood. It's my life. Organizing the people. It's what I do. This is what I believe in. You do understand, Thelma? That's one of the reasons that I value you. You understand a lot without me explaining."

Bobby looked out of the window at the deepening gloom. He turned frowning and said, "In the morning, we do what we gotta do."

The day broke crisp and clear. The wind was blowing from the west. It was a light breeze with a bit of a chill to it. Just enough to make one shiver. Surprisingly, the mood in the room was light as the western breeze. One at a time, Bobby, Thelma, Jason and Tiffenie left the tiny downtown apartment. They darted out onto the sidewalk, head down with a purpose in each step. Each took a different route. Thelma walked steadily. She would have to get used to wearing a wig. It made her head feel hot. With some makeup she had lightened her complexion and donned a light red mushroom wig. Instead of her usual jeans and sweatshirt, she wore rhinestone jeans, with boots and a city version of a cowgirl hat. In her left hand she carried a satchel. The all-important disk was sewn into the inside of her tee shirt. It rested against her left rib cage. In the bus station, police were checking ID's carefully. Sister Clarice had furnished Thelma with a fake driver's license, Social Security card, and a well-worn work ID from a company that had recently gone out of business.

The line moved quickly. Thelma's heart pounded harder the closer she got to the checkpoint. The guard squinted at her driver's license then carefully scanned her face to match with the blurry photo. He entered her Social Security number into a hand-held computer. Her heart almost stopped.

"You're fine, Mrs. Pippen. In about a month from now you'll have to get a travel pass to get from one city to another. All you have to do is go down to the nearest Social Security office and they will issue you one."

Thelma thanked the guard and boarded the waiting bus. It would take twelve hours for her to reach Houston. If all went well, she would be back on a bus headed for New York City within the week.

Fatigued, Thelma leaned her head against the window of the bus. She and Bobby had explored every possible alternative in lovemaking the previous night. Thelma thought that dancing kept her in pretty good shape. It did, but there were some muscles that were used exclusively for lovemaking. Those muscles were sore. Excitement faded to grey highways and telephone poles rolling by her window. Thelma slept, a deep sleep on her ride to Houston. The landscape rolled past, some of it as flat as a pancake. Big Sky Country, that's what they called Montana. Forcing herself, she ate from the vending machines in the various stops along the way. Thelma would zap them in the microwave and thirty seconds later and voila – mushburgers. It was no telling what was really on the sandwiches, but it would have to do until she got settled and could fix herself a decent meal. She stopped herself; wasn't she supposed to meet Bobby? So used to being alone and planning accordingly, she had to pinch herself sometimes for being, as Bobby called it, selfish. Thinking for two was much more complicated then for one. Wonder what ol' crazy girl is doing, her thoughts going to Tiffenie. She chuckled to herself, visualizing Tiff stuffing herself into that little sleeping bag. That's my girl, but she is crazy. The security network at the bus station cut her daydreaming short.

"ID please, Ms.," a grey uniformed guard politely demanded at the entrance. He surveyed her driver's license carefully. Then entered her false Social Security number into a hand held computer. Her heart begin pounding. He smiled, "You're fine, Ma'am. Welcome to Houston."

Thelma claimed her luggage and walked as far from the bus station that she could until she hailed a taxi. Briefly, she thought of Sister Clarice. For some unknown reason, she knew that she would never see Miss Clarice again. What a woman, she exclaimed to herself. Her hand went to the disk sewn into her tee-shirt. She felt the contours of the disk. Satisfied that the disk was secure, she leaned forward in the cab and said, "I need a room. Clean, safe, and not too expensive." The cabby nodded his head.

Thelma returned to her private thoughts. Duty called. She would not fail The Organization nor Miss Clarice.

Houston was a large city spread out over miles. In some areas you thought you were in Mexico; the majority of the people being of Indian or Mexican origin. The cabby took her into an area that was ninety-nine percent Black populated. It was the policy of The Organization that you reside with your people no matter what the conditions. It was the conditions that were to be changed.

How could you change something that you had no prior knowledge of? Much of the information acquired through The Organization's political education classes did not make sense until much later. The instructors always preached that practice and theory go hand in hand. One without the other was useless, or so they would say.

Thelma's room was clean and seemed to be in an area where crime was not rampant. Just before taking her shower, Thelma removed a piece of the worn carpet. She took a razor knife and cut a square into the hardwood floor. Wrapping the disk in a plastic baggy, she carefully inserted the disk in the space previously cut and covered it with the piece of carpet. Thelma walked around the patch in the floor observing her handiwork. Unless you were looking for that circle in the floor, it was difficult to find. Her rendezvous would be in two days. After that she was free to meet up with Bobby and the crew in New York City. She hoped everything would go smoothly. Briefly she thought of Lion and Silvia. What a pair. Their assignment was somewhere out of the country, of that she was sure. Silvia was too hot to be around in the States.

At that moment, Silvia and Lion were stuck in a baggage room at Kennedy Airport. Their prearranged flight had been cancelled because of bad weather. Lion, in a business suit, and Silvia in brown pleated slacks and white blouse, had almost made it onto the next flight.

One of the attendants looked at Silvia more than once. She had on a wig and had made up her face as best she could. Silvia had not figured on an all-out search for her for at least another two days. Then she was sure that the banking authorities in Switzerland, Holland, Germany, Belgium, and Stockholm would unleash their hounds. She had gotten into their privileged computer system and stolen at least fifteen billion. Then she had painstakingly re-coded all first access numbers to the international network. Everything all over the world was fucked up.

Wasn't that a glorious thing to do. That is what Sister
Clarice had told her. She had subverted funds earmarked
for CIA operations in West Africa to orphanages in Haiti
and Jamaica. Naughty, naughty naughty, it felt so-o-o-o-
good. Yeah, they wanted her ass, and bad.

The attendant, uninformed of who he was dealing with,
had her step around a secluded corner. He then pulled a
photocopy of a picture on it from his hip pocket. He com-
pared the picture to Silvia. She smiled and withdrew her
plastic knife and cut him from ear to ear. Blood gushed
out onto his clean white shirt. Except from the gurgling of
the blood, he didn't make a sound. He was even kind
enough to sink to the floor quietly. Silvia stabbed at the
spot where she thought his heart would be. Messing up
her plans. The gall of him, Silvia thought. She beckoned
Lion casually from around the corner.

"We got to get rid of the body," Silvia whispered ur-
gently.

Lion looked left then right. Careful so that he would not
get blood on his clothes, he dragged the body behind some
trash cans. That would have to do.

While waiting in line, there was another delay because
of some new safety regulation. Twenty minutes would be
a lifetime to Silvia and Lion. Sweating bullets, Silvia and
Lion watched as security men burst into the building from
every conceivable entrance. Someone had discovered the
body. Men in bright red jackets lined passengers up in
groups and began questioning them. One of the security
men had retrieved Silvia's picture from the corpse. He
was holding it out in front on him and looking around the
terminal. Silvia turned and buried her head into Lion's
shoulder. They slowly walked toward the baggage room.

There was so much excitement going on that the station,
attendants did not notice them enter the baggage room

behind the counter. Lion stooped behind a large old fashioned steam trunk, standing on end, It was taller than Lion. Lion discovered another steam trunk, though not as large. Silently, he pointed to the large trunk, then at himself. He motioned to the smaller trunk, then to Silvia.

"What are you doing back here, Ms.?" A white-haired flight attendant had come to the back to get a bag for a customer.

"I'm looking for my jewelry pouch," Silvia answered.

Moving quickly toward him, Silvia stopped. Instinctively, the man took a step in her direction. With her left hand innocently out in front of her Silvia stepped in with her left foot. In her right hand, she held the knife close to her hips, shielding it from view. She bent deep at the knee, bringing the blade of the knife upward in an arc. The blade, honed to a razor sharpness, entered the man at the base of the chin and proceeded unhindered up through his mouth. Before Lion could move from behind the trunk, Silvia had struck. Silvia wickedly dug her knife in, then wrenched it away, all in one motion. The attendant fell silently, clutching his neck. Lion shook his head. Silvia's eyes gleamed. Her quickness and smoothly oiled motion was an athletic feat to behold.

"If they find the body in here, they will tear this baggage room apart," Lion stated. Swiftly they searched the baggages for something suitable.

"Wait," Lion whispered fiercely. Finding a large plastic garment bag, he and Silvia stuffed the body in it and zipped it up.

Lion eased his frame into the steamer trunk after he was satisfied that Silvia was secured in the smaller one. Silvia had altered the tags so that both trunks were tagged to the same destination. Flight 74009 took off one hour late, winging its way to Western Europe.

A pencil stream of light entered through a seam in his trunk. Lying in his own excrement, Lion was satisfied that his trunk was on the ground. After being unloaded, the trunk had been bounced around at least a dozen times. Two days without water or food had not dulled the fire in Lion's heart. He was ready to be out and away from here. His trunk had latches on the inside. Silvia's did not. He opened the trunk slowly. He Swayed slightly; the fresh air making him giddy. This is the way vampires must feel after a long sleep, he thought. He did not see Silvia's trunk right away. Lion's search became frantic. He gasped when he saw Silvia's trunk; there was a huge dent in it. Worrying with the leather straps, then wrenching the lock off with his bare hands, Lion removed a layer of clothes from on top of her.

At first glance, she seemed dead. Silvia moved and a gush of air escaped from the still form. Lion pulled her from the trunk. It was about three-thirty in the morning Western European time.

There was a janitor's locker room off to the right, complete with a shower. Lion stripped Silvia, then removed his dank clothing. He found a chair and propped Silvia's nude form in the shower. He washed himself, then Silvia. Silvia came to from the shock of the cold water. Her eyes grew wide at the realization that they were nude and Lion was washing her. Silvia shook her head and mumbled something. Lion nodded and helped her sit down in the chair. He then went and ransacked the janitor's closets and found two sets of clothing. Dishevelled but clean, Lion supported Silvia and they limped to the front of the airport and hailed a cab.

"What the fuck! Denmark!" Lion exclaimed, once he had figured out where they were. He saw billboards around the airport. The cab driver seemed indifferent to their state of affairs. He would never know that it was his total indifference that saved his life that day. They had a problem, their state of dress gained them unwanted attention. Silvia was still out of it. Lion figured that she might have suffered a slight concussion when the trunk was damaged. Taped to their bodies were money belts containing upwards of a half million dollars. Lion had to duck into an alley to get enough small bills to check into a sleazy hotel.

"Silvia, you are going to have to stay quiet until I get us some clothes and food, and you need medical attention. First things first. Silvia, can you hear me?" Lion said, leaning over Silvia's prone figure.

She raised up slightly and said, "Lion, how long has it been since New York?"

"It's been three days. I think that you have a slight concussion. You need medical help. As soon as we eat, I'm going out to get us some clothes. Try to write down your sizes," he said softly.

The food arrived by a delivery boy who tried to push his way past Lion into the room. Lion stopped him by placing a hand on his chest.

"Hold up, man. My woman's not dressed." There was a communication barrier. Silvia spoke enough Swedish to get by, but she was not up to it.

"How much," Lion said slowly. The reddish blonde boy was about Lion's age. His eyes grew wide when Lion displayed a number of bills to choose from.

"I speak English very well," the man said in a halting accent. Lion's eyes narrowed.

"We need some things. Can you get them?" Lion asked.

"Whatever you need. I can get it for you. Drugs, freaks, guns. My name is Hans, he said, offering his hand.

Lion shook it, relieved. Hans would be their ticket.

"Hans, I want you to come back in one hour. I'll give you a twenty now and more later," Lion said, holding the twenty in the air.

After feeding Silvia, Lion realized that she needed immediate medical help. She would be cognizant one moment and out of it the next. He examined her head and neck. There was indeed a large bump on the back of Silvia's head, and her neck seemed slightly twisted.

Ain't that a trip, him meeting a reddish-blonde hustler in Denmark. First some clothes, then a doctor. They would not stay in this room more than a couple of days. The cab driver would remember where he dropped them. Lion's mind sped on. Silvia had hinted that it was much more than money that they carried in those disks. Lion wondered what it could be. What was more valuable than money?

There was a soft knock on the door. Lion took a deep breath and answered, "Yeah. Who is it?

"It's Hans," a voice answered.

After purchasing some clothes, Lion did not feel as conspicuous. When Hans asked him his name, he had told him Jimmy. Luck was with him. Hans knew all of the underworld going's on in Denmark. Lion was not impressed with the doctor that Hans brought to their room. But, he had no choice. The doctor did not speak English, so Hans translated.

"The doctor says that your wife has a slight concussion and that she has suffered from dehydration and exposure. She needs, at minimum, three weeks rest, along with the medication that he prescribed."

"She'll be OK." Hans stated, watching the doctor evenly.

After the doctor left, Lion instructed Hans to get the prescription. Lion waited until Hans had returned and began to dress Silvia. He explained to Hans that they

would need to go somewhere and rest for at least a month.
Their timetable allowed for six months to a year. Their
first objective was accomplished — to get out of the country.

Hans secured a car and took them to the country. He led
them to a cottage set off the road at least a half mile. It
had a green slate covered roof and red painted shutters.
Among the trees and rolling hillside, it resembled a
children's story house that he remembered from grade
school. It even had a white picket fence around it.

He and Silvia settled in. The next leg of their journey
would have to wait until Silvia healed. Lion began to like
Hans and would regret when he would have to kill him.

The recording, *I Want to be Down* could be heard floating
from the streets below. Thelma's body began its gyrating
without her even being aware of it. She hadn't danced in
the last two months. Gazing out of her window, she observed four girls, probably aged fourteen to eighteen,
dancing on the sidewalk. One girl, round, and blue-black
in complexion, was clearly the best dancer. She was doing
the percolator with her own special twist to it. Thelma,
intrigued, joined the girls on the sidewalk for closer inspection.

"Hi, my name is Thelma," she greeted. The girls, apprehensive, approached her warily. "Well. Cat got your
tongues?" Thelma asked.

"Naw. Cat ain't got my tongue. Who you?" the taller of
the four girls asked. The girl was tall for her age with a
sallow yellow complexion. Her glasses were as thick as
coke bottles.

"I was just watching you dance. Will you show me that
step you were doing just a moment ago?" Thelma asked.

"What kind of dances can you do?" the girl that reminded her of Tiffenie asked.

"I'll show you if you show me that dance you were just doing."

"Sandy, put the Snoop Doggy Dog tape in," she instructed. The music kicked off a slow grinding funk tempo.

Despite her roundabout girlish figure, she could percolate and dip on a motion. Not missing a beat, she jumped into a hip hop jig. Thelma jumped in, dancing with her. She added a down drop on every other beat. The girl copied what Thelma had shown her and added something of her own. Thelma threw caution to the wind and cut loose, dipping and grinding while percolating down the sidewalk. Soaked in sweat, Thelma, lost in her own motion, for a moment regained her consciousness to observe the girls watching her with their mouths hanging wide open.

"Whew, woman, where did you learn to do that!" Sandy exclaimed. The four young girls stood spellbound.

"I used to take dancing lessons when I was your age and I practiced a lot," Thelma explained, panting from her exertions. "I'm a little bit out of shape," she added, catching her breath.

"Did you ever dance on videos?" Carol asked.

"No, but it's something to think about," Thelma answered.

The tape stopped and the girls crowded around her.

"My name is Sandy, this is Shanta, this is Carol and we call her Moon," the girl with the coke bottles for glasses introduced the three other girls.

The girl called Moon reminded Thelma of Tiffenie. She was about to tell her this when a woman in her early thirties came walking up the sidewalk yelling, "Moon, didn't I tell you to watch your little brothers." She snatched Moon by her collar and smacked her.

The girl named Sandy said, "Mrs. Rockwood, Junior was asleep. We was just out here a few minutes."

"Shut up, you little bitch, and mind your business," Mrs. Rockwood retorted. The woman with a head rag partially covering her unkempt hair, snatched Moon and dragged her by the hand into their apartment. Moon looked back at her with a pleading expression on her round face.

"If that bitch would quit sucking off all the dope boys on the block for a bump, she could watch her kids herself," Shanta said bitterly.

"You need to check your older sister instead of talking 'bout Moon's mamma," Carol retaliated. Shanta balled her fists. Thelma positioned herself between the girls.

"It won't stop your pain by hurting each other," Thelma said evenly. Shanta and Carol were both crying without throwing a blow. Without knowing what to do, Thelma embraced both girls. They buried their heads into Thelma and cried. There was so much emotional pain in these city streets. Thelma began to understand what The Organization's political education classes meant when they talked about the ravages of a profit-at-all-cost mentality and the psychological effects that it had on the poor. It was the environment that the economics created.

Carol suddenly pulled away from Thelma and began walking down the street.

"Wait!" Thelma yelled.

"Wait for what? You can't help me," Carol said storming down the sidewalk, her form disappearing into the throngs of humanity. Yes I can help you Thelma thought, but it would take time. The girls needed political education. They needed the arms of The Organization.

Back in her apartment, Thelma thought of the work that Bobby was planning to do. Yes, that was a part of her calling, she resolved. Suddenly, she was tired of being alone. Before it had been different, but she needed a family of people around her to make her feel whole.

Old people, young people, babies, teenagers, a culture torn asunder. That's what the inner city produced in too many numbers. Alienated, frightened, angry men and women trying to realize a dream that their conditions prevented them from obtaining. The term 'Cultural Imperialism' brought about a new meaning to her. She observed that these teenagers created a culture that was internationally adopted. It fed everyone but the creators of it. Their dress, style and mannerism, even their slang, was mimicked all over the world. The economic exploitation of the African community spoke to the politically powerlessness of the Black man in America. Categorically, it was he who received the political disrespect. But there were contradictions in every case. It was their time in history to make a mark. Thelma smiled to herself. Bobby was hers. He represented something that she never thought she would have — commitment and permanence in a relationship. This time away from him made her appreciate him more. In just three more days, she would deliver the disk and join her family in New York. "Please God, let everything go as planned," she whispered aloud to herself.

That night, Houston was a city besieged. A policeman shot a young dope dealer early that day. The 15-year-old was dead before he hit the ground. Yes, the youth was armed, but twenty witnesses swore that he was running away. His gun was still in his waist band. Gangs of young

Blacks roamed that particular area, looting and destroy-
ing the local businesses.

It took well into the morning, with an all-call alert from
the city's police department, to bring the disturbance to a
halt. The flames in the distance cast an eerie
shadow-puppet show on her wall. The wail of sirens kept
her from sleeping. Thelma arose from her bed and
watched the flames until they became a dull black smoke,
soiling the morning air.

J ames Kirk, agent in charge of operations, stood slightly at attention. This was just a briefing, a routine procedure that usually was a waste of time. He had all the information that he needed. Agent Brown was blown to so many tiny bits that a closed casket was necessary. The lab boys barely found enough teeth to get a positive ID. Instead of James Kirk stepping up in rank, he was taking his subordinate's place. Orders directly from the President, 'to deal with this organization and all of its components decisively.' He would wipe any vestiges of it off the face of the earth. Unlike Agent Brown, who was prone to emotional swings, Agent James Kirk was a cold fish. The relentless, bloodsucking kind that is rare and hard to find. There was a nationwide search that was being conducted without the fanfare of the mass media. At least three thousand phone tapes were being conducted at that very moment. Airport computers were accessed and drained of information concerning persons who travelled to specific cities at regular intervals. Files were being compiled on ministers, barber shop owners, cab drivers, and especially university professors.

James Kirk was confident that he would find the culprits and crush this thing. He had covered all angles. On the left side of his desk were the index cards of known members of this organization that had enough sense to disappear. Those who did not take the precaution ordered by The Organization and officially disappear, were locked up or under detention. Ankle bracelets gave the criminal justice agencies a lot of room to work. Their advanced computer system helped them to monitor thousands of suspects and detainees everyday without the state having to pay their room and board.

The technology had already been in place. All that was needed was the political will and incentive. If anybody was stupid enough to break the monitoring system of that ankle bracelet... The inner city military community had developed a type of swat team that was called the 'Release Squad.' These men were trained to track criminals within the confines of the inner city. If your ankle code was broken, a team of men would be at your door within five minutes. The small helicopter developed for inner city flying made this possible.

Agent Kirk let the word get out that anybody that would help him get the ringleaders of this organization would be well paid, and that the purge would abate. Yes, Kirk thought, I've covered every angle there is to cover.

He had to laugh despite himself at the expression of those pampered college professors when they were arrested for questioning. At first indignation, then disbelief when they got the real message of their collective lack of power. Kirk was no fool. Yes, Blacks were capable of setting up and running anything that was built. They had helped to develop in major and minor ways almost every piece of new technology developed in this century. Second to the Japanese, they were the most skilled people of color anywhere. Their decision to want real power was historically inevitable.

Kirk was clear. He enjoyed his position of power and would not sacrifice or compromise it for anything. After all, without power what are you? A nigger.

The cold fear that always grips Jason before a 'task' that was as dangerous as this descended upon him. In the darkness he felt, rather then heard, Bobby moving around behind him. Hits were not his thang. Jason was not chosen for 'Chaka' training because of his congenial demeanor. This shit had really gotten wild. It was beyond Jason's imagination. Living this type of life made him appreciate the work of the original founders of The Organization.

They were correct; organization is everything. Without it you're nothing but an animal reacting to conditions outside your control. A conscious human first must understand the environment in which he lives. He must develop strategies and tactics to control his environment in his cultural interest. He must dictate terms and guidelines for dealing with other human beings and be able to enforce it. For it is human beings that affect this world most profoundly. The human can only realize its potential within the human social experience. What separates humans is their culture — which is their history in motion.

This is what The Organization taught and lived. Jason could not imagine living any other life. Bobby called it a 'revolutionary culture.' Jason called it just living. He enjoyed all aspects of the programs except dirty little jobs like this. The house that they were about to invade could be seen atop a slight knoll. Wrought iron fencing, about ten feet in height, surrounded the estate.

Bobby and Jason were accompanied by three other men that they picked up in Jersey. The man they were after was Albert Shanks. Shanks, a Black investor, had been financed by The Organization. Once the investment company had grown and flourished, he had grown contemptuous of the people that had financed him. Instead of

expanding the finance company as was instructed, he had
sold it to the highest bidder on the open market. The
three million that The Organization had fronted him was
sent to an account. His message had been that he had
paid off his debts, made his millions and was through.
Since the purge of The Organization, he had volunteered
information to the financial authorities. Shanks was
determined to keep his hard earned millions and live in
comfort the rest of his life. To safeguard against an act of
revenge, he had fortified his mansion and hired a small
mercenary force to protect him. Shanks would live out the
rest of his life in comfort. Little did he expect it just would
not be a long life. Tonight would be his last if Bobby had
anything to do with it. This was his assignment — to do
Shanks. This, to Bobby, was a personal matter. He had
acted as a go-between for Mr. Miller to this Mr. Shanks.
Shanks obviously did not take them seriously. Jason
stopped and signaled the other men to lay quite. The
three men that were with them were specialists in entering high security buildings and perimeters. Jason lay
prone on the ground and pulled a dart gun from his arse-
nal.

   Silently, a large Doberman pinscher came running
toward the fence from the interior. Jason took aim and
shot him through the chest. The dog fell without a bark.
Another dog, a German shepherd, fell to the same fate. A
contraption, the likes of which, Jason had never seen
before, was placed between the bars, then a manual crank
was used. The machine pushed the fence apart wide
enough for the men to slip through. Jason stayed where
he was; he would be the lookout. Bobby gave him the
thumbs up sign before squeezing through, followed by the
other men.

Although it was three in the morning, Shanks was up
and about. A high-yellow hooker was his entertainment
for the early morning hours. Capré (at least that's what
she called herself) was decked out in a sky-blue leather
pantsuit. The suit fit so tight, you could see the bulge of
her pubic mound. Capré's rear was one of her major assets. Shanks had his hand snugly on one of those assets
while sipping champagne from a goblet.

"Well Capré, how do you like my home?" Shanks asked.
Capré was leaning her elbows on the bar with her
derrière slightly raised. Shanks had taken advantage of
her position and was carefully weighing each globe. She
turned her head slightly to smile sweetly.

"It's beautiful. I know that I would add a touch of flowers
and roses to your curtains and trim. Give it that fresh
woman feel to it. You can tell that a man picked most of
it. It's lovely, but a home needs a woman's touch.
Wouldn't you say? She asked squirming suggestively.

"Yes, I would definitely say." Shanks answered. He
released his hold and walked around the bar to get another drink. Behind his back, Capré glanced at her watch.
She had to get this over with. Shanks paid exceptionally
well but she had to get her son off to school by
eight-thirty. Later that day, she was to attend her son's
music recital. Hopefully, she would be able to get in a
little sleep after she dropped him off at school. She'd
better speed up the action. When he turned around he
almost bumped into her. Capré crowded her breasts into
him. Their kiss ended with a loud wet smack. Capré
embraced Shanks, then led him into the adjoining bedroom.

There was a guard on the roof. Through his binoculars,
Bobby could see that the guard was equipped with night
vision equipment. Every time the guard's head swiveled

in their direction they lay flat on the slopping turf. The last twenty yards was flat. Something would have to be done with the guard. They had been lucky that they were not detected up to this point. To ask for anything more would be foolish. From his backpack, Bobby pulled a box. The box turned out to contain a twenty-two magnum rifle equipped with a night scope and silencer. Settling his elbows comfortably on the slight rise, he took aim and fired. The guard stumbled, grabbed his head with both hands then fell dead. Getting in would not be a problem — getting out would be the challenge.

The glass on the patio door made a slight sound as it was being cut. Bobby crouched in the darkened living room. Music could be heard coming from the hall. He gave the hand signal to follow and glided to the bedroom doorway. Capré, on her back, was waiting for Shanks to get off her. He had an orgasm a minute ago. She shifted to look at her watch behind his head.

"Baby that was really good," Capré cooed softly in his ear.

Bobby was so swift he did not give Capré time to scream. He snatched Shanks off of her and threw him into the wall. When Shanks tried to stand, one of the men savagely knocked him back onto the carpet with his rifle butt. Capré rolled over onto the floor and rose on one knee.

"Don't kill me. I have a son," Capré pleaded, hands raised toward the ski-masked men.

Bobby crouched and brought his face even with hers. "We will let you live if you lay face down on the bed and don't call the police for ten minutes after we leave.

Capré leaped from her kneeling position onto the bed and buried her face in the pillow. Bobby removed his mask so that Shanks could get a good look at the man who then placed three rounds point-blank into his skull. Blood splattered against the wall in globs. Shanks body slid into a sitting position, his leg stuck out awkwardly.

One of the men moved toward the bed, his weapon raised.

"No. She doesn't have anything to do with it," Bobby stated sharply. She won't call for ten minutes. Will you?" he asked the naked, shivering form.

Her voice, muffled by the pillow, Capré answered, "I won't call for ten minutes. Please mister, I have a son." She raised her wristwatch above her head. Bobby motioned for them to leave. Capré looked at her watch. She did not budge for twenty minutes. By that time, the masked men were driving though the tunnel into New York city.

Thelma stood beside the concession stand. She appeared to be deeply engrossed in a magazine that she had just purchased. The Organization was a stickler for exact detail on drops such as this one. She had been instructed to wear a mid-length purple skirt, with a pink silk blouse. Over her head she had an off-red silk scarf. Along with an envelope she had been given, she had verbally been instructed to look for a Black man in a grey silk suit who would engage her in a coded conversation. She looked out into the street through the glass windows. A revolving door was placed in the middle. A man in a grey suit was walking toward her.

"That's the magazine that I've been looking for. Did you buy it here?" he asked, one eyebrow arched.

"Yes. Here at this counter," she answered.

He moved toward the counter with his hand in his pocket as if he was going to purchase the magazine.

"No, don't buy one. You can have mine," she said, handing him the magazine.

"You're sure you don't mind?" he countered.

"Oh no. I'm finished."

The man took the magazine along with the computer disk that she had placed between the pages. He turned and walked out through the revolving door. That's the last she ever saw of him.

On the sidewalk, Thelma's gait turned frisky. Her task was done. She was on her way to New York City. Before leaving her apartment, she changed her appearance. It took her over two hours to style her wig to match the one on the ID card. After securing her travel pass from the Social Security office she boarded the bus to New York. In two days she would be reunited with her family.

"Whew!" Thelma exclaimed, drawing up her face at the stench of the bus station in New York City. Immediately, she headed for a payphone. ...378-9922... While the phone rang, she prayed.

"Hello, Tiff. Yes, it's me. Come and get me. OK, I'll wait, but hurry."

Thelma was elated Tiff would pick her up in an hour. Before the day would be out she would be with Bobby. She started to pace and then stopped herself. Thelma put a quarter in one of those beat-up black and white televisions and went to sleep on some insane talk show.

"Ah-a-a-a-a-a-a, g-i-r-l," Tiffenie yelled, running with her arms spread wide, attacked Thelma before she had a chance to get her senses. Tiffenie had picked her off the ground and was rocking back and forth. Thelma, elated, embraced Tiffenie. Wiping tears from their eyes, the two women loaded Thelma's bags into a late model station wagon.

"It's so good to see you, Tiff." Thelma was lost for what else to say.

The ride home was hectic. There was a accident on the bridge and the traffic was redirected toward Queens. Instead of an hour, it took all of two hours to get home.

"So what have y'all been doing?" Thelma asked.

"We're laying the groundwork to begin the first phase of organizing. Bobby was in charge of the logistics at first, but I have more skill in that area then anybody in this district. So I'm the lead administrator," Tiffenie stated, smiling broadly. It was obvious that she was proud of her new position. She continued, "We have already identified the neighborhood in which we will base our operations. Tomorrow, we will be doing surveys to get a feel for the population, but today is Thelma's day." She squeezed her friend's arm.

Bobby and Jason got in late that night. The house was dark and Bobby didn't know that Thelma was in his bed fast asleep until he eased his frame onto the bed. Bobby had purchased one of those old fashioned beds, with the springs bolted into the wood frames. The bed creaked and squeaked with the slightest weight placed upon its springs. Tonight, the bed played like a symphony orchestra early into the morning hours.

The house that they had purchased had been renovated only on the upper levels. Ground level was just one large room with pillars spaced evenly around it. Worn wallpaper still clung stubbornly to some of the walls. Dressed in jeans and work boots, Thelma, Jason and Tiffenie stood silent while Bobby worked out their work assignments.

"When are we going to begin?" Thelma asked.

"As soon as we're though canvassing the neighborhood," Tiffenie interjected.

Thelma noticed that Tiffenie and Bobby glared at each other, though only briefly. Later that afternoon, they ran off two thousand copies of the survey that they would be using during their canvassing Monday.

"What's up between you and Tiff?" Thelma asked Bobby when they were alone putting the paper in stacks of one hundred.

"Oh, it's one of those administrative decisions that Tiffenie and I disagree on. My position was that we get the office ready first. Her position was that we do all the necessary groundwork such as the surveys. She pulled rank on me. It's nothing for you to be upset about. It's healthy for us to argue and fight over the destiny of our people. Conflict is healthy in the context of something positive. I love Sister Tiffenie, but we just go at each other over policy and procedures. Tiffenie has some serious administrative skills. She is the lead programmer and administrator in this district. It looks like she might be put on the city board. The way things are shaping up, Tiffenie might be on the Central Crew. Tiffenie is a serious worker. She really fooled all of us. The surveys that we're doing now is possible because she has been able to make accurate assessment with the statistics that are available. In a year or two, we will organize some Black students from the local university to develop statistics based on our perception and our reality. A lot of the statistics taken on Black people are taken to eliminate us as a value to this society. The surveys that we're doing is to find out how many men, women and children reside in this area. It will give us information as to the type of health care that's needed, the major source of income and what they deem are their foremost problems. From these surveys we can ascertain the educational level and the overall ideological development of that particular community. After that, we will be able to determine how much money, time and manpower will be needed to solidify this community." Bobby paused.

"Thelma. Have you made up your mind about your commitment to the Long Robes?"

Thelma understood that he had said all of that just to ask her this question.

Thelma drew her fist to her opposite shoulder the way she had seen Sister Clarice do to Mr. Miller. "Yes, Bobby, I'm committed," she answered.

Bobby smiled. Thelma realized that he had not smiled all day.

"I met some teenage girls in Houston," she began. Thelma embraced Bobby holding his arms pinned to his sides. Her lips inches from his. "They were dancing on the sidewalk. We kicked it and danced. Then one of the girl's mothers came and roughed her up for not keeping watch on her little brother. One thing led to another and we all ended up crying. I'm committed, Bobby, but it's not because of you. It's true, you have helped me to develop but my commitment is for the people." She paused, released him and took a step back.

"What can I say," Bobby answered. "I had to know, Thelma," he continued. "It's like I said before we left your city. This is what I do. I'll do this in one form or another until they put me in my grave," Bobby stated, his eyes never flinching from Thelma's. They embraced, sealing their love in a deeper way.

"Where's Jason and Tiff?" Thelma asked.

"They're somewhere around here," Bobby answered.

"Here's Jason's coat. They're still here," said Thelma, walking through the pillars toward the back room.

Suddenly she stopped. Thelma held out her hand, motioning Bobby to be quiet. She could hear somebody sobbing or moaning. The sound was coming from the back room. Thelma removed her gun from her front jean pocket and cautiously approached where she thought the sound was coming from. Piles of sawdust was scattered throughout the lower level. Someone had swept it into piles. Thelma peered around the corner, her weapon held out in front of her. Tiffenie was leaning against a makeshift carpenter's horse with her jeans around her ankles. Jason was positioned behind her. They were having sex. Tiffenie spied Thelma and put her fingers to her lips. Thelma left as quietly as she had entered.

"Dem nigga's screwing. I can't believe Tiffenie and Jason," she reported to Bobby.

He laughed, holding his stomach. "It ain't funny. They had all morning to get it off and here they are screwing around in our office," Thelma exclaimed.

She and Bobby began piling trash and discarded lumber toward the front of the building. Jason came from the rear of the building after another half hour looking sheepish. Tiffenie flounced in not having a care in the world.

"Was you in back organizing?" Thelma asked, trying to sound innocent.

Jason began sweeping up the piles of sawdust acting as if he had not heard Thelma.

"Get a life, Thelma. I like having sex in public places. It's exciting," Tiffenie replied, unperturbed. Tiffenie turned to pick up a piece of lumber and Thelma whacked her on her rear with her open hand.

"Ouch!" Tiffenie exclaimed. "OK, Mamma Thelma, I'm fixin' to pop you," she threatened, dancing around and doing her version of the Ali shuffle. Thelma began laughing and for the life of her could not stop.

The sun shone brightly. The area that they were in was spotted with empty lots and burnt out or abandoned buildings. There was a large housing complex called Liar's Point. It was in these projects that they wanted to establish The Organization presence.

"Hello, my name is Thelma and I am a field representative for the 'Committee for Community Improvement.' There are a couple of questions that I'd like to ask you," said Thelma, peering into a screen door at a young woman with a baby on her hip.

"What kind of questions?" the woman asked warily.

"I'm not a part of the welfare department, the police, or any other agency if that's what you're worried about. This survey will help you and me take control of our lives," Thelma added, her hand of the screen door.

The woman shifted her child onto the other hip and unlatched the door. "How can I control my life?" the woman asked forcefully. She and Thelma were sitting on a plaid couch. The child was cinnamon brown in complexion and had soft fuzzy hair. Her ears had been pierced and she was reaching for Thelma's earrings. Thelma took off one and gave it to the child. The child gurgled and fell to playing with the trinket.

"We, the organization that I'm committed to, have studied our predicament as a race/class of people. We have determined that we control nothing. Therefore, our children are uneducated and are running amuck in the streets. Our community is the target for uninterrupted exploitation by whoever has the organization, money and ideology and will to do so. We are out-organized at every turn. Our solution is to organize ourselves at every possible juncture in our everyday lives. We must first move to improve the quality of life whereever we live. This step will force the struggle to a higher level."

"What do you mean at a higher level?" the woman asked. "By the way, my name is May."

They shook hands and Thelma continued. "Basically, the economics or the relationship that we have with the mode and means of production keeps in a constant state of crises. We have developed a survival mentality that has with it negative norms in our everyday relationships. We are preoccupied with eating, sleeping, and clothing ourselves. Once we are organized around these issues, we can turn our energy and resources toward fighting the system that has waged a relentless war against our culture since we were wrenched from the continent of Africa."

"What do Africa got to do with the projects?" May asked.

"That's a historical process which we will discuss at another time. Briefly, it is a series of processes that got us to this level of existence. We must create a process to get us out of it. Let me try to give you an example. You have a child," Thelma stated. May nodded her head.

"Well, in order for you to have this child you first had to have sex, then over a period of nine months, the child reached a developmental stage in which she was ready to be born. Now in order for you to not have a child, or to have a healthy child, you have to understand the processes."

The woman began nodding her head. "Yeah, I'm starting to understand a little bit, but it will take me time to understand everything that you're saying," May said.

"You think that you might be interested in our political education class?" Thelma asked.

"Yeah, I might, but I don't have anyone to keep Shanay," she stated, referring to her child.

"You can bring the child with you. What we're doing at this point is organizing welfare mothers around the issue of child care. Collectively, we can provide child care and the proper education to go along with it."

Thelma finished the survey and signed May up for the upcoming political education classes. Back on the street she spotted Bobby and Jason talking with some young bloods in an alley.

"You muthafuckas is crazy. Ain't nuthin' about this goin' to change," one of the youths argued. He had a handkerchief wrapped around his head. Dredlocks were sticking out and bobbing as he talked. It reminded Thelma of Jomo.

"Young man. If you think that things are beyond your control, they will be. At least let us work with you long enough for you to be able to transcend your environment," Bobby stated. He was animated. This is the type of discussion that got him going.

"Transcend. What the fuck is that?" the youth asked.

"It means that presently you're stuck mentally. You can't envision anything that you don't see or experience in your day to day life. You have allowed the system's media attack to render you helpless. If you can't see beyond your reality you won't be able to change it. All we want to do is help to develop you and your partners to the point where you will be able to think for yourselves."

"We do think for ourselves," they responded hotly.

"Tell me how?" Bobby asked. There was a pause.

"Like I said before, at least give yourselves and us the opportunity to stimulate some growth."

"We'll think about it, funny gymshoe wearing muthafuckas," the man in the dreg locks stated. He then signaled his friends and they walked the opposite way down the alley. Bobby and Jason broke into hysterical laughter. Thelma did not see what was so funny.

"Dem bloods is something else, ain't they?"

Bobby and Jason slapped hands the old style way, bringing their hands down hard.

Bobby held Thelma's arm, "It has taken a year for us to get that far with them. After they couldn't intimidate us, they quit speaking to us or acknowledging our presence. This is the first time in a year that they actually held a conversation with us. That's progress. We should not expect them to respond to us immediately. After all, we sacrificed them to the educational and the penal system for the last thirty years. You can't expect your children to respect you when you allow their worst enemy to educate them," Bobby said, releasing her arm.

Days became weeks, weeks merged into months their commitment became a life-style.

"Who is going to solidify the young mother's league?" Tiffenie asked.

Sitting around on chairs with the desk attached were Thelma, Bobby, Jason and thirteen other men and women who had accepted the yoke of The Organization.

"I won't do it myself, but I'll see that it gets done," Thelma answered.

"We don't expect you to do it yourself, Thelma. Remember your workers? You have to develop young people to take your place. We've solidified the economic program and it's starting to draw the attention of the folks downtown. So everybody, create at least three buffers between yourself and the hands-on operations. If you don't have the people, it's your fault. The memo that went out on June sixteenth stated all point personnel were to start developing protegees and to train them in your job."

Everyone grew quiet. Tiffenie was on one of her rolls. She remembered every memo, every important juncture at every meeting. That was great, but she expected everyone else to be able to do it too. That is where the conflict came in. Thelma had to give it to Tiffenie as an administrator, she had set a serious standard for organizational people to follow. Tiffenie's concept of structure and timing had them almost six months ahead of schedule. The process of internalization of the ideology into the culture of the masses takes time. That process could not be rushed. Tiffenie sat at the front of the room behind a large oak desk.

"Tiffenie, my block is ready to start gleaning. Who is going to handle Raoff and his crew?" A young woman with her hair straightened to look like Greta Garbo had stood and spoke.

Gleaning meant that the neighborhood had developed to the point that it could declare certain areas 'Liberation Zones.' This classification by The Organization deemed that neighborhood now able to enforce the sovereignty of those zones. Street crime was not allowed and that was strictly enforced. Getting caught selling drugs in a 'Liberated Zone' the second time could mean your life if your head was hard enough.

"We're going to give this assignment to one of our protegees," Bobby stood and said. "They're ready. It's been two years. We've been extremely lucky. It's time for the nucleus to move on," he added, looking around to catch Thelma's gaze.

"Thelma's district is having a block party tonight. So if anybody wants to dance, the gig starts at eight," Tiffenie stated, before adjoining the meeting.

"You coming, Tiff?" Thelma asked.

They were walking side by side down the street. Their work had bore them so much fruit that they had to move out of their original house and turn it over to the community. Thelma and Bobby had a place together as did Tiffenie and Jason. Since Tiffenie had taken over The Organization's city structure, she and Thelma had little opportunity to spend time together.

"Yeah, girl I'm coming. We ain't jumped up since I don't know when."

"Remember how we met?" Thelma asked.

"How could I forget? Tiffenie responded. Their pace slowed, it was good to be in each other's presence.

"It was over the vegetable counter at McGrocery."

"Yeah, and we talked about how the price had gone up on cabbage," Thelma added. She smiled and held Tiff's hand. They walked hand in hand like school girls.

"See you tonight," Tiffenie said before getting in her automobile. It was large and luxurious. She waved at Thelma before she sped off.

Liar's Point had changed physically. There were still areas where drugs were openly bought and sold and violence abounded but there were those small enclaves that were labeled liberated zones. No drugs, no prostitution, no violence. These areas were patrolled by area security guards. Each block had a local resident trained. It was the success of these programs that attracted Special Agent James Kirk's attention. Two long years, and no matter how many of these people they tracked down, vestiges of the structures of the original Organization kept popping up. It was like trying to keep the population of rabbits down. Poison, pesticide, biological, chemical, and outright track down and murder tactics did not deter their population expansion.

Bobby and Tiffenie had been very careful in cloaking their various programs under misleading names. Local politicians and the opportunist ministers were used as fronts. They loved to take credit for something that was perceived as positive. Little did they know that they were being played for the vagabond ignorant hypocrites that they were. In meetings and at various community functions, Bobby and Tiffenie would sometime have to excuse themselves from their presence to keep from laughing in their face. There were two particular ministers, one of Islamic faith and another of Christian denomination, that were exceptionally greedy and crass. They had stood and given an hour long speech, each, of how their very lives were in danger, but they had stuck it out and cleaned up the neighborhood. Tiffenie had almost lost it when the Christian minister had openly taken all the credit for their city-wide literature and literacy program. Tiffenie had whispered in Bobby's ear, "Do you think that the mutha can read?" Again, they had excused themselves to go out into the hall to be able to laugh, holding their stomachs because it hurt so much.

There were a couple of ministers that they had come to admire and respect. These they kept out of harms way, unknowning to the ministers themselves.

Back in her apartment, Thelma took a shower and began to prepare for the block party that her teenagers had organized for tonight. She squinted in the mirror, trying to detect wrinkles. The apartment was deathly quiet. Usually Bobby kept their sound system tuned to his favorite local jazz station. Was she happy? That was the question that Bobby had asked her the night before. Yes, she was happy but something was missing. Thelma had not gotten the feel of the stage and dancing out of her. It

was still there, lurking, waiting for the opportunity to
unleash itself. She smiled. Tiffenie's face and hips were
starting to spread. Thelma did not have to be told that
her friend was pregnant. It was the secret that she was
supposed to tell me tonight. A little Tiff or a little Jason.
Oh God, can we stand it, Thelma thought.

Bobby and she had decided that after they had ground
The Organization into the fabric of this community and
moved on, they would try to have a child. Yes, she was
happy. Extremely happy and would not trade her world
for any other. A little Thelma or a miniature Bobby, could
the world stand it. She smiled broadly at her reflection in
the mirror. The metallic sound of a key turning a lock
caught her attention. Just for a instant, Thelma went into
overdrive. She calmed herself. Bobby forgot his garage
keys again. He was to attend an important meeting with
the street gangs tonight. An unfamiliar hand with a gun
attached to it appeared in her mirror.

"Hey, dancing bitch. Remember me? Good ol' Low
Down," a gravel voice asked.

It was as if Thelma had been submerged in a cube of ice.
She could not move. Beyond fright, she did not feel embar-
rassed being naked in her bathroom mirror. Turning,
Thelma looked Low Down squarely in the face.

"Yes. I remember you."

With his left hand, Low Down traced the scratch marks
still faintly etched in his face. "And I'll always remember
you, Ms. Thelma."

Thelma turned her head and closed her eyes waiting for
the report of the gun.

"I'm not going to kill you, Thelma. I found out about
your organization and what it did for us. If I had known
about it, I would have been down for the people too. Look
at me when I'm talkin'," he shouted.

Thelma turned her head once again to look directly at Low Down.

"If I had been given a chance, I'd have been like Mr. Miller. Yeah, street folks know about what's happening. When I was thirteen, in the dead of winter, my mother woke me up at one in the morning. She told me that my little sister was hungry and there was no money. She gave me my coat and shoved me out the door and told me to get them food and get her a pack of cigarettes. I went out in the snow and I got my mamma and little sister some food. I got her a pack of cigarettes too. That's all I knew, and I been gettin' all my life. I feel, I want somebody to care 'bout me. I want respect. The reason that I'm not going to kill you, Thelma, is that your work helps those kids like me. It gives them another way out."

Low Down disappeared as quickly as he had appeared. Thelma sank to her knees on the cold tile and sobbed uncontrollably.

The music tingled off the sidewalk and city streets. The avenues had been roped off and a mass of humanity had spilled onto the concrete night. Thelma sat huddled with her knees under her. Tiffenie took one look at her and pulled a chair along side. Tiffenie listened patiently while Thelma recanted the previous event.

"Whew girl. Do you think that he'll come back?"

"Naw, that's the last that we'll see of Low Down. But if he found me, that means somebody else could too. It's time that we all get hat. And I say fuck the bullshit, we've done our due. We've planted our seeds. They're sprouting all around us. We got over five hundred thousand left. Let's make a break for the continent," Thelma stated. She looked up into Tiffenie's eyes and said, "I know that you would want your child safe."

"How did you know?" Tiffenie asked, placing her hand over her stomach.

"Yo butt and yo face been getting fat for the last month. It's a dead giveaway," Thelma responded, hugging her knees to her.

They sat on a patio that overlooked the street. Directly below them, a large white tent had been erected. Under the tent was a stage with the disc jockey and his system. The last of the teenagers' dance contest was over and the adult contest was about to take place. Tiffenie grinned at Thelma. She said, "You goin' to dance?"

Without answering, Thelma untangled herself from the chair and walked down the fire escape to give her name to the judges. The lights were hot but oh so deliciously familiar. Thelma had chosen TLC'S *Creepin'* to accompany her dance number. Somethings never change. Her stomach began turning flip flops. The music began throbbing, replacing the flip flop with a fullness. Feet churning of their own will, Thelma cavorted on stage. She broke into a double tempo, combining the African twist with the boogaloo. Hands held out in front of her, Thelma swayed on the downbeat. There was a pause, then the music switched to a faster tempo. This was Thelma's cue to ad-lib. Her thighs shook in unison with her shoulders. She let it all hang out. At the conclusion of her number, there was a hollow silence. Then slowly awakening to what they had just witnessed the teenagers went loco wild, followed by the throng. Applause was deafening. It seemed that the entire city stood and clapped for the next ten minutes. Thelma came back on stage and curtsied gracefully. There was another uproar from the audience. Tonight would be the night she would never ever forget. All her bases were covered, her happiness at that moment could not be measured.

From the tallest rooftop two blocks away, a pair of binoculars witnessed the same performance. "Sir, we think that it could be her." Pause. "Sir, I've never seen anybody dance like that nor have I seen an audience respond as resoundingly as that one. It could have caused a riot. Yes sir, we'll keep all of them under surveillance until you get here," the burly man spoke into the hand held radio.

"Who was that?" his partner asked.

"That was Special Agent James Kirk. Don't get excited yet. He'll be here in five hours. You can meet him personally." He turned and resumed watching the forms of Thelma and Bobby embracing in his binoculars.

"That was great, Thelma. I see why you could draw so much attention," Bobby said, encircling her in his arms.

"You know, Bobby, that's the first time that you've seen me dance," Thelma stated. Bobby held Thelma from behind.

"I got a feeling, baby, we got to get up out of here," Bobby whispered.

They were on the patio overlooking the multitude of people stream toward their homes. Thelma nodded her head. Jason and Tiffenie joined them on the patio. Thelma would remember always their four way salute to the 'Revolution.' Peering into her glass, the amber colored liquid focused her dearest friends and family, Tiff, Jason, and her Bobby.

"Why don't you two come over our house. We have an extra bedroom. Y'all can spend the night," Jason said. Tiffenie obviously had told him of her encounter with Low Down.

"We got some things to talk about," Jason added. The mood, previously so gay and light, turned sober. "Let me get some things out of my car. We might as well ride together," said Bobby.

The ride over was quiet. Thelma leaned against Bobby in the back seat of the car. She closed her eyes.

"I'm out of shape, 'cause I'm tired as hell," Thelma mumbled to Bobby. He hugged her to him briefly.

The surveillance team that had been assembled at the last minute was delighted. Instead of four different teams, following four targets, they were all sitting cozy in one automobile. Orders were to detain targets until the special agent in charge arrived. While the four trooped to the elevator, an anxious array of men and vehicles surrounded the block. If one of these targets got away, somebody's head would roll. All involved resolved that it would not be theirs.

Thelma carefully retold the incident concerning Low Down. Bobby slowly shook his head. The four of them were sitting around an oval coffee table. The polished top reflected their profiles.

"OK, we all know that it's time to go. The question is when?" Jason asked.

"A couple of days at the most," Bobby answered.

"Y'all got me so paranoid we can go right now." Tiffenie stood and gestured with an out-flung arm.

"How are we going to divide up the money?" Jason asked.

"Just divide it four ways," Bobby suggested.

"It ain't that important. There's enough money here for us to start another operation somewhere else and still retire," said Tiffenie.

"Five hundred thousand is a lot of money, but it ain't all that," Bobby retorted.

"I don't know if y'all brain dead or what. We've been financing the opening of Black businesses. They're starting to pay us back. Plus, I did some slick Silvia shit down at the banks. I invested some. We'll come out of here with at least three million easy," Tiffenie said, her hand arrogantly on her hip. Jason looked at her and smiled.

"That's my baby," Jason said smiling.

"Are we going to split up?" Thelma asked suddenly. It had dawned on her that Jason and Tiffenie may have other plans.

Tiffenie looked at Thelma, then at Bobby and said, "Not."

"We'll go to the continent, no telling what kind of damage we can do if we ever do want to come out of retirement," she said simply. "Before I forget, let me give y'all something," Tiffenie said while leaving the room. She reentered with a small square box.

"Here, Thelma, Bobby and Jason." Tiffenie handed out money cards. "If anything happens and we're separated, these cards can get you money. That's anywhere in the world where they have international money cards. Sister Silvia clued me in on some discrepancies in the money system that we can take advantage of. So don't lose your cards," she stated, pointing her finger at each word.

"I'm exhausted. Where's the bed?" Thelma asked.

"Y'all's bedroom is in there. We'll see you in the morning. I'm tired too," Tiffenie said, faking a yawn and winking openly at Jason. He rolled his eyes to the ceiling.

"That's why you knocked up now," Thelma admonished, her eyes twinkling.

Thelma was asleep as soon as her head hit the pillow. Bobby lay awake wondering if he could have held up after coming home to see Thelma's brains blown all over the bathroom.

"Let's send out for breakfast," Tiffenie suggested.

It was eight-thirty in the morning. This was a late morning, for their work demanded them to rise at the crack of
dawn. Thelma was leaning out on the balcony. Behind the
complex was a low-income housing project. A maze of
wooden fences wove through the tiny backyards.

Thelma turned to get Tiffenie's attention. "You see those
fences?" she asked. "There is a maze that runs all the way
to the other side. Some of my teenagers showed me while
we were doing surveys in this area. You don't have to go
to the sidewalk to get to the other side."

Tiffenie turned to get Jason's attention. He and Bobby
were in a deep conversation on the far side of the room.
Seeing that it was hopeless, she turned to Thelma and
said, "Why don't you maze your butt over to the breakfast
house and get us some breakfast?"

"Walk with me. It will be fun," Thelma suggested.

"I got some stuff to punch in on the computer. We'll go to
the park after we eat. They're in one of those impossible
ideological discussions, and no telling when that will end,"
Tiffenie said to Thelma.

Thelma's hand was on the knob of the front door.

"Don't go that way. If you know the way through the
project maze, go down the side stairs. You won't have to
walk around the building," Tiffenie suggested.

The staircase that Tiffenie suggested wove its way from
the inside corner of the patio. Thelma was at the bottom
rung when the signal from Special Agent James Kirk was
given to storm the apartment. The door flew from its
hinges, the force knocking the large oak door to the floor.
Jason started up from a sitting position and drew his
weapon on pure instinct. He got off two rounds into the
first man before machine-gun fire ripped him to the floor.
Bobby, his weapon drawn, used the other side of the
heavy couch. He got off at least ten rounds before a shot-

gun blast knocked him to the floor. Tiffenie, coming out of her bedroom with a comb in her hand, was shot point blank thought the throat and stomach. She fell without a sound. The sound of gunfire was immediately followed by a barrage of heavy machine-gun fire. The drone of helicopters caused Thelma to duck under a garbage stand. In a instant, her world of completeness was destroyed. A part of her wanted to believe that somehow Bobby had survived. Reality told her different.

Thelma ran, knocking her knees against mislaid garbage cans. She stopped to catch her breath. Somewhere behind her were her pursuers. More helicopters were filling the air. Men in black fatigues were being dropped into the projects by ropes from the choppers. Agent Kirk was hard to please; three targets were accounted for and one was missing.

"How the hell did she get out of that apartment?" Kirk asked, his voice calm. It was his calm that intimidated Sgt. Cooper.

"After we searched the apartment, we discovered a stairway leading down from the patio. It wound around to the back, that's why we did not see it from the street. The complex was surrounded. She must have left just as we were closing in," he answered, staring at a shiny spot on Kirk's head. He dared not look him in the eye.

"Find her. Tear those projects into pieces if you have to." Kirk looked up from his desk. "Why are you still standing here? You're dismissed," Kirk stated in his flat tone.

"Lion, Lion, wake up." Silvia stood above his sleeping form. The cottage had only one bedroom. Lion slept on the couch in the L shaped front room. He peeped one eye just above the end of the blanket.

"Why are you waking me up, Silvia? There's nothing to do besides sleep and eat," he said, rising up into a sitting position. He yawned, stretching his mouth to cave-like proportions.

"I'm feeling much better and it's time to scoot. We've been here four months. It not cool to stay in one place this long. The guy that usually delivers our groceries has not shown up in two days. My experience tells me that when the routine is broken it's time to go."

"OK, I'll call Hans to get us some transportation to the train station," he responded.

"You are going to cut our losses. Aren't you?" Silvia asked.

"We don't have to do Hans. If it wasn't for him we would be sitting in a cold jail cell. Or you dead if he had not gotten us a doctor."

"Quit crying like a little bitch. It's not fitting for a lion," she retorted.

"I heard that you was cold. But this time it ain't necessary," he shot back. Silvia crossed her arms, still standing over Lion. He tried to stand. She pushed him back to on the couch.

"Look Lion, by now I'm one of the most hunted persons on earth. They know who I am and are offering some serious money to anybody that can finger where we're located. Last time your good friend Hans visited, he barely looked you in the eye, or didn't you notice?"

Lion, a bit puzzled folded his arms across the rippling muscles of his chest. Hans did act sort of different the last time that he visited. In fact, he did not stay as long as he usually did.

"He did act strange," Lion admitted, biting his lower lip. He paused. "Well what do you propose we do?"

"Get packed. Just the things that you need. Toilet articles. We're going to hitch a ride to the city, do your friend Hans, and steal a car. Then we'll catch a train to the coast and get a boat or plane to West Africa. It's simple, Lion, don't make it complicated." She rubbed his head but he knocked her hand off.

"I ain't no dog," Lion complained.

"No, you're my little cubbie bubbie," she replied.

"And you, my dear Silvia, is a stone trip," Lion smiled.

He and Silvia had developed a sibling relationship. She, the older sister and Lion the brother. There were certain things about Silvia that he did not understand. Once, when he had tried to have sex with her, she had let him disrobe her and just lay there looking at him with that fixed stare. Lion had gotten up and gone into the other room. Silvia cackled like a witch. That afternoon he apologized.

"Don't apologize, Lion. It's me that should apologize to you. I was just messing with you. I don't have sex. I don't mess around. It don't work for me. Excitement, doing naughty deeds, that's what gets me off. I love fine clothes and jewels, but it's for that place in me where nobody can come and hurt me."

Silvia had joined him on the tiny front porch. She walked out onto the grass and spun around holding her arms away from her body. The way little kids do when they want to make themselves dizzy. Spinning around, she stopped in front of Lion. "Beside Miss Clarice, you are the closest person to me. My little Brother cub."

Lion was touched. He hugged Silvia to him. Briefly — just a squeeze — she returned the hug. Lion released her quickly. He realized that for Silvia that was one hell of a show of emotions. Since that time, they had grown closer.

They were lucky, a truck driver picked them up as soon as they got to the main road. He dropped them off in the center of town. It was obvious that he was interested in Silvia. His eyes kept dropping to her white-stockinged thighs. If he only knew, Lion thought.

"Well, well, if it isn't Lion's dear friend, Hans," Silvia cooed.

She had a small caliber gun pointed inches from his temple. They had surprised Hans. He was sitting in the kitchen drinking coffee when Silvia and Lion invaded his apartment.

"Don't he look guilty to you, Lion?" Silvia asked.

"As a matter of fact, Hans, you do look guilty," Lion stated.

"You are my friends. Why would I turn you in?" Hans said, stammering over the words. Perspiration had formed on his forehead.

"Now who said anything about anybody turning us in?" Lion asked, grabbing Hans by his golden hair. He twisted it so that it bent Hans' neck at an awkward angle.

"The grocery boy asked about your wife. It was he who told me that she is wanted and that a large amount of money would be given to whoever turned her in," Hans responded.

"So what did you decide?" Silvia asked, shoving the pistol closer to his temple.

"I like Lion. I was going to give him part of the money and let them take you," he said to Silvia.

He looked to Lion, pleading with his eyes. Lion reached into his belt, put the nine millimeter automatic to his head and pulled the trigger. The large round ripped the top of Hans' head off. His body fell to the floor trembling. Silvia savagely kicked the corpse. Lion observe that gleam in her eyes just like at the airport when she wasted the attendant. Lion unscrewed the silencer from the large pistol and put it into his pocket.

The Copenhagen Metro sped straight from the city though the interior of the country, all the way to the opposite coast. Silvia had made herself up to look much older. She had stuffed pillows and pillow cases around her waist. Lion was amazed. Walking though the train terminal, she even talked and moved like an elderly person.

"You so good, I'm about to start calling you Auntie," Lion whispered in her ear.

They were seated in a coach that was almost empty except for an elderly couple that kept smiling at Silvia. Silvia smiled and leaned her head on Lion's shoulder. Lion shifted to get more comfortable. She had fallen asleep.

Twilight descended quickly in this part of the world. Soon the only landscape that Lion could decipher was snow covered peaks far in the distance. From the streets of urban America to this. Wow, he thought. Silvia started to snore softly. He shifted his weight again. Silvia woke up to snuggle closer. Lion smelled her hair. He loved this strange woman. Their bond was something he'd never envisioned. Truly this was his sister. The train howled uninterrupted on into the night.

The route ran straight to a commercial port. This was what Silvia was looking for. There were captains of ships who she knew would transport anything or anybody for a price. Just before getting off the train, Silvia dressed back to her old self.

"Look Silvia, you've recovered from your injury, but you are still not one hundred percent. You seem to be sleeping a lot. So take it easy will ya?" Lion asked.

"I'll be fine, Lion. It's just that I keep getting these terrible headaches. Remember, when we find this guy, let me do the talking," she warned.

For weeks Lion and Silvia hung out on the docks and in bars watching and listening. Finally, when Lion had about given up, a dredlocked Jamaican entered the bar where they were hanging out and ordered a rye and beer. Lion had to nudge Silvia to alert her. She was nodding off in her chair. Sliding on the stool next to the man, Silvia ordered the identical drink. Lion observed from the far table.

"Hey, Captain," she greeted.

The man squinted at her in the dim light. His eyes widened. Furtively he looked around the bar. No one was paying them any attention. He downed his drink and headed for the door. Silvia followed, giving Lion the sign to stay put.

Lion looked at his watch. They had been gone over two hours. Anyplace else in this country, he and Silvia would have stood out like a sore thumb. But on commercial docks the world over, the human population is as diverse as the goods that they're transporting. Silvia appeared at the doorway after another hour. Lion swiftly followed her form into the night.

"What's up," he asked as soon as he had caught up with her.

"We're boarding tonight. We're to meet him on pier 14, dock 3 at two in the morning. He trusts the guy on watch that time of the night," she answered.

Suddenly, she slowed and grabbed her forehead. Lion caught her by the waist. If not for his support, she would have fallen. Back in their hotel room, Lion had her lay down and he placed cold towels across her forehead.

"I think that we had better get you to another doctor," he stated, sitting beside her prone form.

Silvia mumbled something then went to sleep. Lion looked at the clock. It was twelve-thirty. In a hour and a half they would be on a ship heading for West Africa. Going to Africa meant something to Lion, but he still did not know what. Sister Clarice had told him that it would be going full circle. That he would find his complete self. Silvia had read him poems by Countee Cullen and Langston Hughes about what Africa meant to them. It had stirred something deep and mysterious inside him. Still, he could not fathom the significance. It was one-thirty.

"Silvia, hey butter head, wake up." Lion shook her gently. When she was fully awake, it seemed that Silvia was her old self. Lion breathed a sigh of relief. The night air of the sea was frigid cold. The chill seeped through whatever clothing you had on to your very bones.

The captain, overly anxious that they would be seen, rushed them across the gangplank. Their cabin room consisted of a narrow bed and a smelly bathroom.

"I guess I'm supposed to sleep on the floor," Lion mused.

"Naw, we can share. But, it's too narrow for both of us at the same time. I'll sleep on the floor every other night. How about that, my young cub," Silvia answered, while playfully boxing him in the stomach.

"I was just kidding. It don't bother me. I'll feel much better when we see a doctor that speaks English." Lion held her hands to keep her from punching him.

The cargo ship was christened *The Flying Eagle*. It was privately owned by the wild looking Jamaican. It steamed out of the harbor into belligerent waves. In a couple of days, Lion got used to the rolling of the ship under his feet, but Silvia kept throwing up.

Halfway into the voyage, Lion had his first experience with the anger and power of the sea. A storm, bellowing in from the east, caused the ship to pitch and roll against the powerful currents. When Lion thought that all was lost, the ocean calmed to a shimmering glass blanket. Out on deck, the stars shone clear and bright.

"It's simply gorgeous," Silvia stated.

She had slipped up behind Lion who's attention was somewhere in the heavens. Startled, he whirled around. Silvia cackled, a version of Miss Clarice's laugh. She stood next to him grabbing the railing with both hands.

"Miss Clarice had another Lion. His name was Henry. He was a good soldier but he fucked up."

"What did he do?" Lion asked.

"He and four other guys raped two girls. The girls were only fourteen or fifteen. Miss Clarice called him into her office and shot him dead."

Lion looked at Silvia to be sure she wasn't kidding.

"Miss Clarice was something else," he said.

"Miss Clarice saved me, Lion. She saved you, too."

Lion did not reply. He just looked at the stars and the rolling sea.

"What's up with those disks? The ones that you said were more important then money," he asked.

Silvia leaned against Lion briefly, then said, "Twenty-five years ago, there was this teacher in Chicago that opened up her own tutoring classes right in the middle of the south side. After a couple of years she noticed that there were certain types of African kids that had some type of supernatural powers. Well, she wrote research journals about these special children. The Organization found out about it and sent Miss Clarice to investigate. The Organization set up a screening panel. This panel went all over the inner cities in the United States and located kids with these special powers.

Well, to make a long story short, a lot of money was invested in these youngsters. They were sent all over the world to get the best training and education possible. On one of these disks, are the names and locations of the kids that were trained and developed by The Organization. They are called the 'Pyramid Children'. Collectively, they are supposed to make a major contribution to our people. How, I really don't know, but it is essential that these disks get to the Commissioner in Ghana."

"Sometimes I wonder what the fuck I've gotten myself into," Lion stated.

It was hot, the pavement sizzled under ones feet. Lion wiped the sweat from his brow and helped Silvia across the gangplank. Well, so this is Africa. The port was a large bustling one. Ships of all sizes and shapes were anchored in its harbor.

"Be very careful of what you say, Lion. There is as much danger for us here in Africa as there was in the States," Silvia warned.

"Silvia, most of the time you give the orders, but this time I'm calling the shots. Let's deliver these disks first. Then you are going to be checked in to the nearest hospital."

To Lion's surprise she did not protest. After making a series of phone calls he and Silvia caught a cab to a small tavern.

A man in a gleaming white agbada met them there. Silvia handed him the disks and introduced the two.

Mr. Siasad, the Commissioner, after hearing Lion's explanation of Silvia's condition, would not allow Lion to check her into a regular hospital. He said that it was too dangerous. His assurance of the quality of the private hospital on the outskirts of town caused Lion to eye Mr. Siasad suspiciously.

The equipment was modern and the hospital was spotless. The decor did nothing to dispel the fear that gripped him when the doctor would not meet his gaze. Something about a tumor. Realization that he was scared shook him. 'The Lion' had never really feared anything. Silvia was a window through which he saw a different world. She had shown him how to hope. Now to be without her…

Thousands of miles away, Thelma stuck her money card in a CMT machine. Sure enough it spit out a thousand dollars. It was her teenagers who helped her get out of New York. They had hid her against her wishes. She had been transported by car from New York to Houston. Houston hadn't changed much; it was still extremely hot and oppressive. Thelma switched from hotel room to hotel room. Most of the time she stayed in and slept. Every morning when she woke, she wept uncontrollably. It became a routine until the pharmacist at her local drug store prescribed her some valium. Peace was temporary. No matter how many pills she took, when she woke, the pain of losing Bobby, Tiffenie and Jason cut into her like a knife. Thelma contemplated suicide. More times than she cared to remember, she had put her pistol to her head. Cursing her weakness, she'd throw the gun to the floor. Thelma could not go though with it.

Anguish was her only companion. One day, frustrated, Thelma threw the bottle of pills out of her fourth floor window. Three days and two nights she wrestled with her withdrawal from uppers and pain pills. Sometimes it felt as if it was tearing her insides to ribbons. One day, waking up in her own sweat, the tears did not flow. It still hurt but she did not cry. Weak and a little disoriented, Thelma showered and stumbled down the sidewalk to the local fish joint. Sliding into a booth in the back, Thelma raised her finger and ordered, "I'd like a perch fish dinner."

"Is that for here or to go?" the waitress with the coke bottle glasses asked. With her white uniform and starched white hat she could pass for a nurse. Thelma peered up at her from under her denim flop hat.

"Oh, Ms. Thelma, is that you?"

Thelma pulled the front flap of the hat back exposing her face to the warm afternoon sun.

"You seem familiar," Thelma stuttered. "Dancer, you were one of the girls that was dancing under my window."

"Yeah, I'm Sandy. Whew, I'll never forget you. You a for real dancer. Still to this day I ain't seen nobody better." She paused chewing her bubble gum the way cows chew their cud. "Ms. Thelma, you been sick?"

Thelma was at a loss for what to say. She had not given a thought to her appearance in months.

"You ain't on that caine is you?" Sandy whispered, her eyes wide with dread and concern.

"Naw, I ain't on nothin', Sandy. I've had a rough time. I mean I been real sick," she corrected herself. The last phrase was but a whisper. She winced with pain.

"I got a little money if you need some, Ms. Thelma," Sandy offered.

"No, I'm fine. I really need that fish dinner though."

"Right away, Ms. Thelma. Wait 'til I tell Shanta and Carol that I saw you."

"Shanta and Carol are the girls that were with you that day?" Thelma asked.

"Yeah, and Moon was with us too," Sandy replied.

"Where's Moon, Sandy," Thelma suddenly asked.

Sandy looked around the empty restaurant before answering. "Moon got herself mixed up with Spandex. Her mamma owe him some money and Moon trying to get him off of her mamma. Spandex is a mighty bad man. I wish I was a man, I'd shoot that low life mutha," she stated vehemently.

A stirring flash of fullness, erupted in her stomach. Thelma rose from her seat. "Bring Moon to me tomorrow. I'll write my address down before I leave," she commanded.

Eating slowly, Thelma felt her strength returning.

The next morning, the splattering of rain wakened Thelma. She rose quickly and showered. Carefully, Thelma surveyed her reflection in the mirror. There were dark circles under her eyes and her face was gaunt, but no wrinkles. The pain returned to her. The agony of grief was blunted by this new task she had undertaken. Taking a deep breath, Thelma started to dress.

"Come in," Thelma answered to the hurried knock on the door. Four girls and a young man entered the apartment, shaking the rain from their clothing. Thelma sat on a couch that was against the wall. Dark granny glasses adorned her face. Thelma gathered herself and stood.

"And who is this?" she asked.

"This is Paul. He's cool. He don't like Spandex neither," Sandy answered. "You're not mad that I brought him are you?"

"Oh no. We can work with Paul. I'll need all my children around me." Thelma paused. The words, 'her children,' had come out of her mouth of their own accord. Moon stood just behind Sandy, she too was wearing dark sunglasses.

"Come here, Moon," Thelma stated.

Moon moved stiffly toward her. Behind her dark glasses was an unsmiling face. Thelma reached to remove the dark glasses from Moon. Moon resisted, Thelma was insistent and, after lightly slapping Moon's hand away, she removed the sunglasses. Her left eye was badly swollen, and there was a cut under Moon's cheek.

"Who did this, Moon," Thelma asked.

"Spandex did it because I would not perform sexual favors for him or his crew," Moon answered, her voice flat.

Thelma folded her arms. Silence followed.

"We goin' to deal with Spandex. Tell him that I have his money. I want you to bring him to me, but I want it done late at night," Thelma stated. Her attention turned to Paul. He was squat with a barrel chest and weight lifter's thighs. "A young bull in our mist," Thelma commented smiling. "Would any of you like some breakfast and tea?" The smell of bacon and eggs wafted through the apartment.

"Mrs. Thelma, you don't know Spandex; he might do anything. I ain't even told you how much money I owe him," Moon protested. Thelma casually waved her hand, not answering.

Later that night, Moon gave the coded knock on the apartment door. She entered wearing a skintight red dress and black heels. Moon was scared, but there was something about Ms. Thelma that gave her confidence. A man in his late twenties was with her. He wore expensive jeans and gym shoes and had a thick gold chain around his neck. Thelma looked into his eyes, cruelty seeped out from the corners.

"You got my money?" he asked abruptly.

Thelma walked to the door and looked both ways down the hall. She reentered the apartment and locked the door.

"I got what you deserve," Thelma stated. She raised a small pistol to his head and pulled the trigger four times. He fell, his body twitched then lay still. Moon leaned against the wall in shock. Thelma coolly raised her window and signalled. Paul entered the apartment carrying a duffel bag. He unzipped the bag and pulled out a military body bag. She and Paul stuffed the still form into the bag and dragged it into the bathroom.

"We'll get rid of the body later, first we have to get paid," Thelma stated.

They left her apartment and entered Spandex's vacant home with his key. After a half hour search, a stash of money and about a kilo of cocaine was found. Thelma flushed the drugs down the toilet and gave Moon the rest of the money. Paul and Moon had not spoken since Thelma had killed Spandex in her apartment. They waited wide eyed for her next command.

"Moon, I want you to go home and pack. You're going to stay with me awhile. Paul, you and I have something to do. Did you get everything that I told you?" she asked.

"I got everything, Ms. Thelma," Paul answered.

It was three weeks later that Sandy and Shanta entered Thelma's newly purchased house.

"Why did you get a house so big?" Shanta asked, going from room to room.

"We'll need the room. You'll understand after awhile," Thelma responded.

Before Shanta left that day, she turned around to say good-bye. Thelma was sitting in a straight back chair. She had a long silk granny dress with gold buttons down the front. On one side of her stood Moon, on the other side stood Paul. Both had their arms folded and stood like statues.

"Bye, Mamma Thelma," said Shanta. Shanta hesitated, "Are you going to teach me how do dance?" she asked, her hand on the door knob.

"Of course I'll show you how to dance. All inner city kids should know their steps," Thelma answered.

Shanta her hand still on the door knob paused.

"Good day, my child," Thelma said.

Shanta closed the door softly behind her.

10,000 miles away, tears slowly gathered in Lion's eyes and flowed a trail down both cheeks onto the floor. He sat and sobbed. Silvia had died on the operating table. The tumor had gone too far. That's what the doctor had said. The man to whom they had given the disks patted him on the shoulder.

"There's nothing more you can do, Lion, she's dead." He paused. "Come with me, young man," said Mr. Siasad.

The white bronco left a trail of dust behind it. They were on a road that led to a vast plateau. Antelope and wildebeest dotted the vast planes. It was the dry season; the animals of the savannah were on the move.

Lion and the man got out of the jeep. Stretching his arm out, the man pointed at the vast unending plain.

"Your friend Silvia told me that you're quite a runner," he said.

Lion, confused, nodded his head.

"When you're hurt and confused what do you do?" he asked.

"When I was at home, I'd run uptown and back," Lion answered.

The man pointed at the vast plain. Lion's pulse quickened. He started to trot, his feet raising clouds of dust with every step. His stride elongated, his arms became pistons driving his legs to a faster pace. From where the man stood on the road, the figure of Lion became obscure with the blowing dust. A herd of antelope raised their heads from their feeding, sniffing the air. As one, they pirouetted and ran with the wind. Thousands of hooves drove a whirlwind of dust into the swirling wind. The oldest predator scent had been picked out of the dust — it was the scent of The Lion.

THE END

Watch for Upcoming
Books from
Donald E. Dukes
to be Released...

"MILKDOG"

"SUNDIPPED CHILDREN"

"BEYOND THE FURTHEST STAR"

"IN THE SHADOWS
OF THE GREAT PYRAMIDS"